GATES ALONG MY PATH

Karen Board Moran

For my grandchildren,
Jared Weston and Jocelyn Laura Moran.

May they always be curious.

Gates Along My Path

ISBN 978-1-300-61764-8

TABLE OF CONTENTS

Uncovering Stories from the Past

This manuscript became the author's inspiration to bring the 1850 Worcester children to life. Like any manuscript, the information is subject to human error and interpretation, but it helps lead researchers to additional sources of information. One can see the entire Worcester Children's Friend Society Records, 1849-1921 by requesting Call Number: Mss. Octavo Vols. W.

AUTHOR'S NOTE

While reading the minutes of the Worcester, Massachusetts Children's Friend Society at the American Antiquarian Society in 1997, I "met" the orphans of 1850. How could I help the children of today hear the story of the children of Worcester across the centuries? I hoped readers could become time travelers much as I experience when I do research in original manuscripts.

This young adult historic fiction novel is my attempt to unlock the past. It is impossible to know the spoken words and details of the lives of individuals who lived in the past unless they kept a journal, wrote letters or were quoted in some document or newspaper. By using many primary and secondary sources, I hope this book will help the reader revive a sense of how the children growing up in the dynamic Worcester [woo-ster] community of 1850 are not so different from the children of our time. While none of the children were famous enough to have books written about them, their posterity lives today—six generations later.

I've done my best to capture the variety of ways different characters spoke at the time. Passages from personal writings are quoted as written or as I imagine they would be written. I've used the language of their time and backgrounds, including words that may no longer be acceptable in today's society. The Appendix will help readers with 19th century language and to in find the actual locations of the story on a period city map. See the Bibliography to learn where you can discover more about the historic characters.

I invite you to climb through this window on the past to join the children of 1850.

Karen Board Moran

1 January 2013

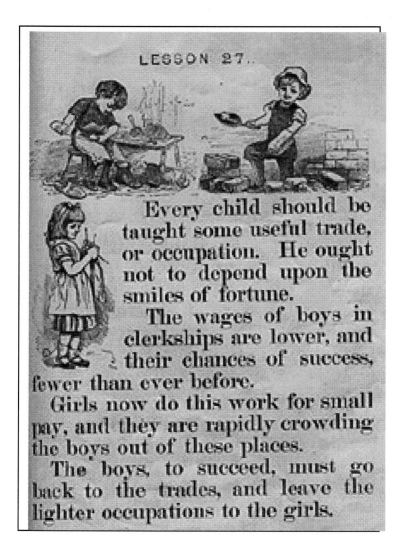

LESSON 27.

Every child should be taught some useful trade, or occupation. He ought not to depend upon the smiles of fortune.

The wages of boys in clerkships are lower, and their chances of success, fewer than ever before.

Girls now do this work for small pay, and they are rapidly crowding the boys out of these places.

The boys, to succeed, must go back to the trades, and leave the lighter occupations to the girls.

A lesson from, *The Home Primer*, a mid-19th century children's reader found at the American Antiquarian Society, Worcester, Massachusetts.

"Out of the Mouths of Babes". Women's History Workshop.
<www.assumption.edu/whw>.

,ott Mill in Lowell, Massachusetts c. 1850.
National Historical Park; Kirk Doggett, Illustrator.
.gov/nr/twhp/wwwlps/lessons/21boott/21visual2.htm>.

NEW YEAR'S ESCAPE

' Street Station

,cester, Massachusetts[1] January 20, 1853

"Liza[2], stop wiggling!" Mary cautions. "You'll attract attention."

---

[1] Worcester [woo-stir] is located in the center of Massachusetts about 45 miles west of Boston.

[2] Liza was born in Ireland about 1842 as Eliza McLoughlin. She is listed as living at the Orphan's Home as Eliza B. Lochlin, aged 8, in the 1850 Census taken in September of that year. It is believed she was one of the McLoughlin children accepted by the Children's Friend Society on 29 December 1849. Sometimes Americans gave orphans non-Irish sounding names or the census taker wrote down what he thought he heard. Mary Locklin, 19, is listed in the 1850 Census living with the Miles family and born in Ireland. The Children's Friend Society still exists in 2012.

How could my sister expect me to sit still as we are suddenly enveloped in a swirl of smoke and steam? The noisy train had finally pulled inside the Foster Street station. For a brief moment hidden by the fog I felt safe, but then ghostly figures began to emerge as the Monday morning crowd of passengers hurry to their destinations around Worcester. I am truly trying my best to act grown up like my 22-year-old sister Mary who's almost twice my years. She seems fearless. Isn't she afraid of taking this bold step?

Colored Lithograph of Interior view of Foster Street Station 1855. Black and white version in *Ballou's Pictorial Drawing–Room Companion*, October 20,1855 (249). Courtesy, American Antiquarian Society.

My thoughts keep wandering from the adventurous expectation of today's escape to fear in a matter of seconds. Am I making a terrible mistake? I must have courage. I have made my decision to go through the gate offered by Mary. I am tired of others leading me down paths they choose for me. I am old enough to choose my own!

Oh no, here comes another crowd of disembarking passengers who scan the crowd for friends and family. Will Mary see anyone she knows? Or worse, will someone recognize her?

Mary must be thinking the same thing for she stealthily lifts her pretty blue plaid dress over our dark green carpetbag. Now, it's safely inside the hollow formed by her hoop. She looks innocent as she studies her gloved hands with bowed head. We look like we are waiting to meet someone, rather than traveling. But I spy trouble as Mary's elegant new bonnet demurely covers her dark auburn hair. Its spring-like pink roses keep catching the eye of men and women alike. She is so proud of her American look. Could it be our undoing?

I try to calm myself by remembering how Mary had boldly walked to the Ticket Office to purchase our tickets to Lowell just an hour earlier. She paid our $2.50 passage as if it were an everyday occurrence. I was so proud of her. Just think, it was almost two weeks of her wages.

She has met so many people while working for the Miles family over the past four years. Surely, we shall be caught! Even sitting in the Ladies' Waiting Room, we are in danger.

Perhaps, we will be captured because of me. Someone may have already reported seeing me in the train station. It certainly won't be on account of my beauty. I'm hardly noticed next to Mary's self-confidence and womanly grace. Short and swaddled in my dark brown dress, woolen plaid cape and quilted green bonnet, I feel like a walking carpetbag. At dawn I donned every stitch of clothing I own for the five-mile winter's ride into town. Thank goodness I finally finished quilting a heavy petticoat. The bitterly cold weather makes it necessary for everyone to bundle up, too. I doubt the suspicions of my master were aroused in the pale morning light. Mr. and Mrs. Burbank think I'm just spending a winter's day with Mary in Worcester.

Earlier, as we walked up to the station, I thought we were done before our adventure had begun.

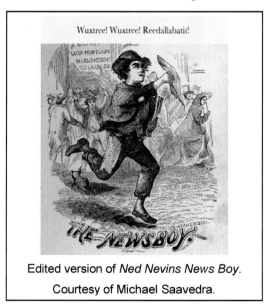

Edited version of *Ned Nevins News Boy*.
Courtesy of Michael Saavedra.

"Papers! Papers! Liza?!" Jimmy yelled in his loud newsboy's voice, the words echoing and heads turning our way.[3]

Jimmy and I have been friends almost since the day I arrived at the Orphans' Home three years ago.

"Shhh! I am running away," I whispered, clutching his arm while Mary stood back.

With a quick nod he had promised to say nary a word to anyone even if they asked. His indenture with Mr. Earle at the *Worcester Daily Spy* began about the same time as mine had with my master Mr. Burbank. However, he was pleased with his contract. He hoped to rise from newsboy to journalist. He gave me a wink of support as we entered the station. There was no time to explain further.

Are Mary and I doing the right thing? I feel like a traitor. Mother Miles and the Children's Friend Society have given me so much. Then last fall I turned eleven. I was forced into indenture with the Burbank family in Shrewsbury to learn domestic skills and no longer be a burden.[4] I was considered old enough to earn my way until I turned 18. Younger, more helpless children needed my bed at the Orphans' Home. I guess I should be grateful the managers found me a place so close to my brother Tom and my sister Ellen, but did anyone

---

[3] Jimmy is listed as James Nolan, aged 7 in the 1850 Census, so he could have been indentured on his eleventh birthday, but his specific indenture is not mentioned in Children's Friend Society ledger.

[4] Eliza's first indenture is unknown.

ask me what I wanted? No! I had been so happy at the Home where not a day passed where I learned new ideas and helped the wee'ns.

Mother Miles, founder of the Children's Friend Society. Hale's *Worcester in 1850.*

At first the Burbank family had seemed kindly. The Board of Managers was pleased during their inspection visits, but not I. I soon discovered the work was so burdensome that I seldom could stay awake to continue my studies. No one listened to my dream of becoming a teacher. Then just last month Mrs. Burbank crushed my hopes with her stern words. "Schoolin'? You don't need any more book learnin'! Irish lasses should stay in their place and catch a good lad of their own kind to take care of them." I kept my peace with Ma's frequent reminder in my heart, "The Blessed Lord would never close one gate without opening another."

Luckily, I didn't have long to wait. Mary's friend Bridgy sent a Christmas letter from Lowell.[5]

> *…They pay in hard cash for a 6 day week, 12 hours a day. The rest of the day is yers, Mary.*
>
> *Tis not difficult ta learn yer task on the machine. Nothin back breakin like doin floors. Come board with me family in the Acre.*
>
> *The company wants lasses like us cuz Yankee girls complain an cause trouble.*
>
> *There be more Irish lads here than lasses --with much better finances than ever on the ould sod…*

Mary has been eager to leave Worcester ever since Richard announced his betrothal to Miss Weston. Heartbroken, Mary already considered herself a spinster. "I'll spin in the mills and build my own nest egg," she had firmly declared. "No master or mistress will determine MY future. I'm going to the

---

[5] Lowell, Massachusetts, a city created to produce textiles- cloth and thread or yarn- was known as the "City of Spindles". A spindle is a round stick used to twist the fiber into thread or yarn. In 1853 the fixed workday was from 7 a.m. to 7 p.m. Monday through Friday, but only until 4:15 p.m. on Saturdays. On Sundays the mill girls were required to attend church. The Acre neighborhood was created by Irish immigrants.

City of Spindles. Come with me, Liza, and break free from the domestic path."

"But what do the Yankee girls complain about?" I had asked after we reread the letter. I figured there had to be a problem if they actually wanted foreign girls like us.

"Don't be a ninny, Liza. Yankee girls are pampered and lazy. Mother Miles was always praising the hard workin' Irish lasses -- even tho' she complained about my papist ['pā-pist] beliefs. I want fixed hours and some certain time to myself. Hard work for hard cash will help both of us find new gates to open. Look how far I've come from the crop failures and epidemics in Ireland. There, my only choices were to become a nun or leave. We're blessed we do not have to turn our wages over to a father or husband. It's time to move on!"

I had been amazed that Mary had asked me to join her. Up to now, people always were telling me where to go and what to do. Now an unopened gate was before me. I was finally given a choice. Stay or flee? I decided I could save the money earned in the mill to attend a nearby seminary. Perhaps I could even earn enough to go to Mt. Holyoke or the Framingham Normal School. Bridgy had mentioned many girls attended the Lyceum after work to improve their mental development. I will not always be a factory girl!

Winter Morning in the Country
Currier & Ives Christmas card, 2000.

It seems ages since Mary had arranged for the McLoughlin family to celebrate the New Year together at mass at St. John's Church. Mr. Knowlton had graciously allowed my brother Tom to borrow his sleigh to bring Ellen and me over the freshly fallen snow. Joyously, we had ridden through the crisp air across the floating bridge on Lake Quinsigamond. We had celebrated our freedom from chores on the anniversary of our arrival in Worcester just three years ago when Tom and Ellen began their indentures.[6] On our way we had stopped to treat the children at the Orphans' Home to a brief sleigh ride.

Our happy spirits, however, had been dampened after mass when Mary shared her plan for the two of us to leave Worcester in the new year.

"How can ye even think of movin' ta Lowell?" Tom had lectured. "'Tis sweating inside the mill how ye want ta spend

---

[6] In the 1850 Shrewsbury Census, Thomas Lochlin, 12, lives with Mr. Mark Knowlton and Ellen Lochlin, 12, lives with Ms. Hannah W. Noyes. All names used within various households are from Census lists.

your day? Where will ye live? When will Ellen an' I see ye both again?"

"Be fair, Tom," Mary had quietly answered. "In Lowell Liza and I will be free to choose our place of worship. Isn't that what this country's about? I'm tired of being a servant. I want to be on my own, not at the beck and call of Mrs. Miles. Some Yankee girls complain about millwork, but a day's pay for a day's work is what I need. Now my day never ends. I'm no longer behold'n for Liza's upkeep at the Orphans' Home. We will be able to see you in less than three hours by train. Perhaps some area farmer might even let you deliver their goods to the Lowell market."

Tom loves the rolling green farm fields and team of horses he helps tend. In three years he will be free to have a farm of his own. He doesn't mind facing the whims of nature. Unlike farmers back in Ireland, Yankee farmers grow a variety of crops like Indian corn, oats, Irish potatoes and hay. They also raise swine and cows and keep a large orchard.

How could he ever understand our need to move? Tom has never been housebound like we girls. He often delivers apples, potatoes, cider and butter to the Worcester markets. Mr. Knowlton even took him to the Cattle Fair in Worcester and the Mechanics Fair in Boston last fall. He's allowed to keep a penny for every leather shoe sole or load of wood he cuts after finishing his regular chores. His greatest regret is that he's not allowed to hang around with other Irish lads. How would he ever understand our need to move?

"Lasses shouldn't be off on their own," he had stormed. "Look at th' Irish lads at mass today. Why don't ye just find a husband an' take care of Liza? And Liza, shame on ye for not givin' th' Burbanks a chance ta help ye learn th' skills ye need ta be a good wife! Look at how well Ellen is doin'."

Poor Mary! Tears had filled her eyes, but she had tried not to cause a scene. Her beau's family had forced Richard into a marriage with a local girl rather than allow him to marry Irish. He hadn't loved her true or he would have followed his heart. Mary had worked so hard trying to sound more American in her speech and dress. In fact, I think Tom was most angry about her dropping the old ways.

Suddenly Ellen had distracted us with an outburst. "Thomas McLoughlin, ye have no idea what me days are like! I dinna ever get ta leave th' farm 'cept for school. At everyone's beck and call am I from 5 year-old Sally ta the ailing grandparents in their eighties. Widow Noyes allows me no peace from dawn ta dusk and beyond. I dream of headin' west ta th' gold fields with Sandy next year. His brother has inherited th' farm and is treatin' Sandy more an' more like a hired hand. Ye be leavin' Mary and Liza ta findin' their own way. I, too, wish I had more energy ta continue me schoolin'. Da an' Ma could do no more than sign their names. I'm lucky Widow Noyes still allows me ta attend winter school sessions."

She had squeezed my hand and whispered, "I don't think anyone will chase ye ta Lowell, Liza."

Western engine house, Worcester,   Courtesy, American Antiquarian Society.

CLANG! CLANG! CLANG!

"All-l-l-l aboard!"

I nearly jump out of my skin. The 10:30 Boston train preparing to leave interrupts my memories of Ellen's reassurances and Tom's angry words.

Mary's hand gently touches mine. "Can you believe that engine, called the "Lion," was the first locomotive in Worcester back in 1835? Why, 'tis older than you."

Her words help me take in my surroundings until we can board the Nashua cars just before 11 o'clock. I am not expected to meet Mr. Burbank until four this afternoon, so I must relax. May God have mercy on our souls.

Mary is doing the same thing and tries to keep me occupied. "Do you see the woman in the dark blue bonnet over by the second tracks? That's Abby Kelley Foster.[7] She lectures all over the country against slavery and for a woman's right to speak in public. Do you remember hearing about her speeches?"

"Who're the man and little girl waving good-bye to her?"

"Oh, that's her husband, Stephen, and their little girl, Alla. He also lectures, but feels Abby is a better speaker. Some call her 'the Queen of our female reformers.' Can you believe he stays at their farm in Tatnuck and cares for Alla? I think Richard would have been that kind of supportive husband. Mrs. Miles, however, was always commenting on how wrong it was for a mother to leave her child. However, Alla certainly needs no Orphans' Home." Mary adds with a sigh.

"I think we must live our convictions, Mary. My teacher, Miss Gleason, told me Mother Miles also used her eloquence to enlist the sympathy of the community to start the Children's Friend Society. She and Mr. Miles even opened their home as the first Orphans' Home. How can she criticize another reformer?"

"It's always easier to find fault than to give someone praise, Liza. Everyone has different talents and must find a way to use them to help themselves and others. Some people say the Fosters could grow rich with their commanding talents if

---

[7] Abby Kelley Foster (1811-1887) and Stephen S. Foster (1809-1881) are both radical abolitionists living in Worcester in the area now called Tatnuck. Their house on Mower Street is on the National Historic Register. Their daughter Alla was born in 1847.

that was their goal.   The Massachusetts Anti-Slavery Society pays Mrs. Foster a salary to help pay their farm bills.   Their farm is openly called 'Liberty Farm' because it is part of the Underground Railroad.   My friend Molly works for them and says Mrs. Foster treats her very fairly."

At center: Frederick Douglass, Garret Smith and Abby Kelley Foster at Anti-Slavery meeting in Cazenovia, New York, August 1850. Sterling's *Ahead of Her Time* (preceding 117).

I wish I could act as self-confident as Mrs. Foster. Imagine traveling alone on the cars to strange cities! She must be so brave to speak in front of crowds of men and women mixed together.   Miss Gleason told me people even threw things at Mrs. Foster for speaking before such promiscuous audiences. Men become upset when a woman does not stay in her place—and often so do other women.   Now, many people will be upset with Mary and me for leaving what they consider our place—Irish servants. Every year since I came to this town, there has been a convention to discuss woman's rights. If Mrs. Foster and other strong-minded women did not challenge traditions, everyone would be stuck in "their" place. Mary has certainly been encouraged to think about what is best for her, not what others think is "her" place!

I guess that's what helped me decide to run away. Ma often said when God opens a gate along one's path, we have the power to go through it or walk on by. She cautioned the choice was seldom easy to make and to ponder it a while, rather than rush through.

I also find it strange that many people do not think slaves should be free, even here in the North. Last summer my friend Becca told me how her aunt Betsey escaped to freedom in Canada. There are black and white people here in Worcester who help the fugitives escape, even though there is a strong law against it.

Oh dear, some might call me a fugitive from my indenture. When the blacksmith's apprentice ran away, Mr. Burbank told his wife, "Some think that servitude clause in the Fugitive Slave Law applies to runaway white apprentices, too." Well, I certainly have been serving like a drudge the past three months! Almost as a slave since I was placed against my will and can no longer attend school. What will be my punishment if I am caught?

The more I ponder the situation the more I decide I'll be brave like Mrs. Foster traveling alone to a strange city. I'm escaping to freedom, but also reforming my life. Why shouldn't I be allowed to keep the money I earn? I should be able to save enough to go to school. Why wasn't I allowed to choose my life's work? I detest keeping house and cooking. I would rather read and learn of new things. Satisfied with my new-found courage, I scan the station crowds.

"Merciful heavens, Mary. There is Henry Rawson!" I whisper, scrunching down on the bench. Hopefully, he's too busy to recognize me and tell his mother. She serves on the Board of Managers. Mrs. Rawson will be just one of the many people angry and disappointed because I'm breaking my indenture contract. Miss Gleason often reminded us this was one of the few contracts females are legally allowed to sign. The managers had had to work very hard to convince the state legislature that the female managers were capable of acting as guardians for the children whose fathers didn't accept their legal rights to their children. Still, it was a contract to be enslaved by one's own consent! She and Miss White would debate the fairness of this type of work agreement for hours, but felt it better for the orphans to be in a situation that provided a good home and training. The Children's Friend Society could not afford to find foster homes or care for every child until they turned eighteen. Knowing no better, I had accepted the fact that this was my lot in life, just as both Ellen and Tom had three years ago. At least, that was until I myself was bound to work I did not choose.

"How much longer, Mary?" My nerves are making me hungry for our lunch of hard-boiled eggs, bread and apples. I haven't eaten since dawn. My stomach growls in a very unladylike manner.

Mary frowns with that "grow up" look. "The next train is ours. It goes to Groton Junction where we catch the train to Lowell. It won't be long now."

She tries to capture my attention again by pointing out a woman with the brown shawl over her head and three wee'ns. "Doesn't she remind you of Ma when we landed at New York? How confusing this strange land was! Ma told us to sit quietly and observe what is going on before setting forth on the next leg of any journey. Even after five years, I miss her so."

"Well, no matter what happens, Liza, we're still better off than if we had stayed in Ireland. The famine has only worsened. Da was determined to make his way in America. Now, it is up to us." We silently hold hands and watch a man return to gather his family and leave the station.

Silent tears tickle my cheeks, but stop instantly as the bench and ground vibrate. The squealing brakes and hiss of steam bounce off the walls. Jostling and chattering passengers disembark from the train continuing to Groton Junction.

We gather our carpetbag and I clutch my kerchief tightly. It holds all my meager possessions and our lunch. Can we cross the tracks to board the Nashua cars without being noticed? Engulfed by the crowd of tall adults, I feel very insignificant waddling along and begin to sweat in a very unladylike manner. At least no one can see me very well.

The nice smiling conductor helps me climb aboard and I can breathe once more.

As I reach the top step, a groan escapes Mary's lips. Her hand presses into my back to shove me forward into the car.

"Hush, Liza! Don't look back!" whispers Mary. "Git as far up front as you can and scrunch down. Don't look up until I come for you.

As she turned to find a seat in the next car back, I find the very front left seat in the car empty. I try to make myself invisible beneath the seat.

Oh, Ma and Da. Why did you have to die? We surely will be caught!

Where'er thou journeyest, or what'er thy care;
My heart shall follow, and my spirit share.
Mrs. Lydia Huntley Sigourney

An Irish Gate. Courtesy of Wikimedia Commons.
<http://commons.wikimedia.org>.

A GATE CLOSES

Trying not to cry, I escape into my memories. Could it only be three years since Mary and Mother Miles had met us at this same station? Fear makes me like a little girl again, waiting for Ma and Da to save me. I find solace and courage in my memories of those terrible last days in New York. I barely remember the details of the day Da was killed in a construction accident in New York City.

Father Paul had come to Delancy's crowded Sixth Ward tenement to tell Ma. My life would never be the same after that fateful day.[8]

New York City   December 1, 1849

"His will be done, Liza," Ma quietly whispered in my ear. "Do not cry over what canna be changed." She wiped away her own tears and hugged each of us before leaving us in Aunt Kate's care where we continued to sew on shirt buttons to earn a few more pennies.

No one could spare a moment's earning power. Since I turned eight, my job was to watch the wee'ns as they pulled threads off the finished shirts. I barely understood Da wouldn't be coming home ever again. Tom and Ellen had told me the sad story later.

The neighing shrieks of horses, screams and clanging bells reached our ears even in the back rooms on the fourth floor. Tom ran down to see what the commotion was all about.

Sobbing new tears atop the dried ones for Da, he slowly returned up the stairs to report more tragic news.

In her haste with tear clouded eyes to go claim Da's body, Ma had not seen the carriage passing a heavily loaded

[8] According to the Board Minutes in the Ledger, three McLoughlin children were accepted on 29 December 1849. In the 1853 Annual Report (page 10) tells of a runaway "little girl, was one of three orphan children, who came from Ireland, three years since, in a most forlorn condition...their expenses from New-York [sic]" had been advanced by the society since their sister lived with the Miles family.

wagon on the icy cobbled street. None of us had ever become comfortable with the bustling roads of this huge city. They were constantly filled with people rushing past in all sorts and sizes of carriages and carts with warning bells clanging. The noises all jangled together amid the dirty snow.

A carriage horse had knocked Ma to the ground. The wheel had crushed her neck. Weakened by 'sumption, Ma had not been able to jump out of the way fast enough. She had never been the same since our long trip 'cross the ocean. Weak and wheezing for breath, Ma could barely climb the four flights of stairs to our room. She seemed to be shrinking before our eyes.

Oh, Ma! Why did you and Da have to leave us alone in this strange country? I know you would say, "Look for God's next gate to open along your path." Practical Da would say, "Work hard and save yer pennies." But death slammed the gate shut on the McLoughlin family. We were orphans, alone in a huge city.

Father Paul helped us bury our parents and wrote to Mary, our older sister. Mary had moved to Worcester, Massachusetts, shortly after we arrived in New York City, to make her own way in America.[9]

_____

[9] The Potato Famine from 1845-1860 forced nearly two million people, or a quarter of the Irish nation, to seek refuge on America's shores. Many middle class Yankee families looked for Irish girls as live-in domestic help. Having few expenses, the girls usually sent most of their wages to their families. Irish men often found work digging canals and building railroads. As soon as

Excerpt from Coffey's *Irish in America* (39).

Da constantly reminded us that the freedom of America made it possible for every citizen to become wealthy. We just had to keep our eyes open to opportunities and seize them.

On the boat over, Mary had befriended Bridget Moran and her wee daughters, Winifred and Mary.[10] I often played with them on the deck to keep myself busy and escape the smells below decks as the ship pitched and rolled. Their da worked on the railroad in a town called Worcester. Da was impressed with the success of a fellow Irishman who had started out digging canals. He suggested Mary help the Morans travel on to a place called Massachusetts so Mary

---

they had enough money saved, they often sent passage money to bring their families to America to start a new life together.

[10] The Moran family from Ireland was listed in the 1850 Census, but no other details are known.

would have a chaperone. Me heart broke when Mary left us, but now there was more room in the bed.

We lived with the Delancys. Uncle Pat had passed away of pnnmony of the lungs. Aunt Kate's only income was the piecework she did at home stitch'n men's shirts while watching her four wee'ns. She needed our family's help. We all went to work on collars or buttons depending on our abilities. She needed every penny Da gave her for our lodging to pay her rent. It was a lively household with the eleven of us squeezed into two rooms. I didn't much like sharing a cot with Ellen and my two squirmy little cousins, but we had no choice.

Tom contributed the pennies he earned as an errand boy for the sweatshop next door. Ma frequently said, "'Tis counting your blessings you should be," whenever Tom wanted to go off on his own to escape the crowded apartment. Now he says those same words to me. Doesn't he remember? He was only eleven like me now? I, too, am eager to be on my own way.

He and Da often argued about the freedom they had hoped to find in this democratic country. "Proud and happy ye should be ta be away from where the county charges a man when he's down," Da would sternly remind him. "They impounded our cow an' dinna care if the taters 'twas infected with blight, the bean with fly an' the cabbage with black beetle."

I can barely remember the old life in Ireland, but I remember when there was no longer milk to drink and little to eat. I had worried about what would we do without Ma and Da.

Then the letter came from Mary with tickets for Worcester!

Worcester Children's Friend Society.

This Society has been organized about one year, and has received a charter from the Legislature. Its object is to " rescue from evil and misery, such children as are deprived of the care of their natural parents "

Through the liberality of John W. Lincoln, Esq. a comfortable asylum has been provided on Pine Street, where children are received. Mrs. J. M. Miles, 26 Chestnut St is Superintendent.

Howland, Henry J. *Worcester Almanac Directory for 1850* (15).

Luckily Mary was boarding in Worcester with the Miles family on Cedar Street in exchange for her domestic help. Mr. Miles was a carpenter who had three children. The youngest, 3-year-old Abby, still needed much attention, and there was also a boarder who worked with Mr. Miles. Mrs. Miles was busy with her duties as superintendent of the Children's Friend Society. Mary admired "Mother Miles", as she was fondly known.[11]

Mary had told us of how Mother Miles had boldly visited the abodes of poverty and wretchedness along Pine Street and

---

[11] Anstis Kendall Miles (1789-1885) founded the Children's Friend Society in 1849 after witnessing "the sad spectacle of children receiving their earliest lessons of household education, from the example of immoral and intemperate parents." The organization continues to help children in Worcester today.

Green Island for over a year. Then she tried to enlist the practical sympathy of others to help "poverty-stricken human beings [and] friendless young creatures who present themselves in all their ragged wretchedness before us." She finally was able to organize the Children's Friend Society for "the protection and education of destitute children." At first she kept the orphans in her own home, but soon needed a separate Orphans' Home. Having live-in household help freed Mother Miles and other fine ladies for benevolent work.

Mary often told me the story of how she had tearfully shared Father Paul's letter with Mr. and Mrs. Miles just before Christmas that year. They advanced ticket money for the three of us to leave New York City. In exchange, Tom, Ellen and I would be given up to the Society's care. Of course, I didn't understand this at the time. Mary's only concern had been to protect us and reunite our family. She worked hard to pay off the $12.00 debt for the tickets.

We said a tearful farewell to Aunt Kate leaving Ma's kittle, smoothin' iron, and bed clothes with her in hopes she could take in other boarders or sell them. All three of us were poorly dressed for the cold trip north, but had little choice. We layered the few clothes we owned to stay warm. Tom donned

Da's cap as the new head of our family. Ellen wore Ma's gray woolen shawl with the flecks of purple and gold that reminded all of us of the wild flowers of home. She carried Ma's shoes in her brown pocket-handkerchief. One of us would soon grow into them.

Ellen gave me her old gray threadbare shawl to add to mine. My job was to carry the oatmeal cakes for the journey. Merciful Lord, after our ocean voyage I thought we would never have to eat so poorly again. Even Aunt Kate's cabbage soup was preferable! Thank the Lord, we would be with Mary the next day. I knew our big sister would save us.

Steamer *Connecticut*, second of the name, went into service Norwich to New York, in Nov. 1850. Shown at the N&W dock at Norwich. Courtesy Connecticut Historical Society.

Farnum's *The Quickest Route* (before 53).

Even in our sadness, it was quite an adventure to take the evening boat from New York City to Norwich, Connecticut. The gentle roll of the waves on Long Island Sound was very different from the heaving swells on the open ocean. Ellen said the ship was a new steamer called the *Connecticut*.

Ellen and I curled up on the hard benches near the stove for it was very cold, but not yet snowing. We didn't even notice Tom had left us to explore the ship for we immediately fell into an exhausted sleep, rocked by waves.

Tom discovered the large paddle wheels on either side of the steamboat were connected to large cylinders housing a moving piston. The pistons were attached by connecting rods to a crankshaft at right angles to the cylinders. As steam was admitted to the cylinder, it pushed the piston forward forcing the paddle wheel to turn around its large axle. This type of power required the coal fires to be constantly tended, so the water was always boilin' in the large tanks to produce continuous steam. At least six sweating men fed the furnaces all night.

In the morning I told Tom the paddles reminded me of the grist mill's water wheel back home. "Yer a bright colleen, Liza. The wheels harness the water's power just like Da harnessed our horse. The difference", he explained, "is the grist mill's wheel is pushed around by falling water, but the paddle wheeler pulls itself forward through the water."

My brother is very smart, even if he smelled of oil and was covered in coal dust!

For the next part of our journey, we boarded the Worcester cars. They were pulled by an engine with the strange name of *Uncas* painted on its side. There are so many strange words in this country! We listened to a lady telling her little boy that Uncas was an Indian chief who became famous when James Fennimore Cooper wrote a book called *The Last of the Mohicans.* I wondered if there were Indians near our new home? Ellen said maybe when we learned to read, we could read this book to learn more about Indians. And later I did!

Norwich and Worcester first No. 5, *Uncas,* built by the Springfield Car & Engine Co. in 1850. Courtesy Freeman M. Fogg, Stoughton, Mass.
Farnum's *The Quickest Route* (before 53).

After overcoming our initial fears of this noisy, smoke-throwing machine, we peered out the windows at open fields even though the cold air found its way inside. We had not seen the like since leaving Ireland. There were many more trees and snowy fields in America. Tom's hopes began to rise. He had hated the city and dreamed of one day owning a farm.

Tom was fascinated with how the locomotive worked and had asked the engineer a million questions before the train pulled out of the station. It had pistons, too, and two big wheels on either side of the engine. He chattered away most of the three hour trip comparing the steam ship to the train engine. These pistons pushed the wheels forward and pulled the train cars behind the powerful steam engine. He informed us there was only room for one fireman to feed the coal from the coal car into the firebox, but at least there was fresh air compared to being below decks on the steamboat.

"Liza, th' marvels of this new industrial age will be openin' many gates for new invention. Someday I'll be able to pull or push me plow with a steam engine."

Personally, I didn't like the noise, smoke and cinders of this marvel, but it certainly was fast. My face was almost glued to the window, but I never saw a single thatched roof cottage like ours back home. Ellen reminded us of the fun we all had had helping Ma thatch our peat cabin. How Ma had laughed! Those memories gave us strength to face the fast approaching unknown.

Tymeson's *Worcester Centennial. 1848-1948* (frontispiece).

As the train pulled into Worcester, we realized this town was smaller than New York City. In the cluster of homes and smokestacks, the train passed a large building on a hill. The conductor told us it was the College of the Holy Cross, a Catholic college. I hoped the priest would be as kind as Father Paul. On the other side we saw a strange stone tower on another hill. The conductor muttered, "Don't see why girls need a college, let alone one that looks like a castle. Do they think they're princesses? "

Oread School in *Gleason's Pictorial*, 19 March 1853.
Courtesy, American Antiquarian Society.

A third large building several stories high and capped with a dome loomed upon yet another distant hill. At the time I wondered aloud if we would live there. Then I was shocked when another passenger said it was one of the largest buildings in this state and full of lunatics and idiots.

Original asylum c. 1847. Opacity, Urban Ruins. <www.opacity.us>.

Just before the train stopped, it crossed a large snowy area someone called "The Common". Lonely gravestones were sticking out of the burying ground with no fence or wall to protect this white field surrounded by many buildings, including several churches. Happy I was that Ma and Da were buried safe within the walls of the church yard in New York City.

The train pulled right into a station building that looked like a Greek temple in a picture Da had once showed us. What a strange and wondrous place, I had thought at the time.

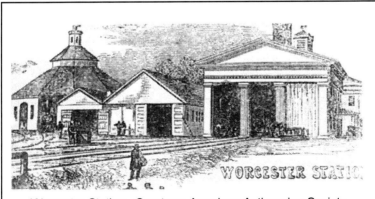

Worcester Station. Courtesy, American Antiquarian Society.

No wonder these memories flood into my head at this terrible moment as I now try to leave Worcester. May God have mercy on our souls.

O is for orphan, for which thousands are made,
Every month in the year, by the Rumseller's trade.
"Temperance Alphabet"
Massachusetts Cataract and Waterfall

People "need not waste their sighs and tears,
and unproductive sympathies, upon imaginary objects,
while there is so much actual misery in real life."
Children's Friend Society
First Annual Report
January, 1850 for year of 1849

Barnyard gate on Freegrace Marble farm,
Sutton. Massachusetts. 2002.

"I wish you a happy new year!"

How different Mother Miles' countenance will be if we are caught today compared to four years ago! Back then she was my salvation as we had prepared to begin the new year down new paths.

Worcester, Massachusetts   December 29, 1849

The McLoughlin family was together again! Joyfully we entered the Miles' home on Chester Street.[12] How different it was from our crowded tenement in the city and our thatched roof cottage in Ireland. Mother Miles warmly greeted us in her sunny carpeted parlor that smelled of pine boughs brought in for Christmas. Blessed Virgin, her kindly brown eyes reminded me of Ma.

Her daughter Louisa, however, ignored us and continued playing with her little sister. I hardly noticed as I was drawn to the shiny black horsehair sofa in the opposite corner. Mary grabbed my arm to stop me from sitting on it. I had wondered why someone would have such a beautiful thing if people were not allowed to sit on it? This was one of my first memories of being treated differently.

"Don't ye be worrying 'bout Miz Louisa," Mary whispered as she hurried us into the kitchen. "She's angry with her ma for spending so much time helping others. She can be vain and selfish. Today, she must care for Abby which is usually part of my responsibility."

Later, Ellen said Miss Louisa reminded her of the shopkeepers in New York who put signs in their windows that said, NO IRISH NEED APPLY. I soon discovered that some

---

[12]According to the 1850 Census, Jonas M. Miles, 51, and Anstis K. Miles,51, lived at 26 Chestnut Street at Williams Street with their children: Eugene L. Miles (24, born in MA and a clerk), Louisa K. Miles (16, born in NH and not attending school), Abigail B. Miles (3, born in MA).

people tried to ignore or wish away those who are different to avoid trouble.

A wonder awaited us before the kitchen fireplace-- a large tin bathing tub. It fascinated even Tom. We had a cuppa tea and hot buttered toast while Mary heated water for our baths on a large cast iron stove. The tub was so big!, We could sit in it and slide under the water. Tom loved it, but I did not want to drown.

19th century tin bath. Object Lessons.
<objectlessons.org/houses-and-homes-victorian>.

Sweet smelling lavender soap was truly another unexpected New Year's treat. Mary trimmed, combed and braided our clean hair as we renewed our family ties. Tom did not even complain at the attention--Mary so reminded us of Ma.

To our great surprise, we each were given a clean set of clothes and our worn rags disappeared. Tom was given a tan woolen shirt, dark brown linsey-woolsy trousers and vest, a red cotton neck-cloth called a bandanna, and a heavy dark green wool coat. He tried to argue about wearing the knitted undervest and drawers Mary had made for him so he could work comfortably outside. America was such a strange place, for none us had ever worn under drawers before! My pantalets even had a ruffle along the bottom edge.

To fight the New England winter, we each received a warm wool scarf, gloves, shoes and woolen stockings. Tom also was given a gray knitted woolen cap. Ellen and I were delighted with our green print quilted hoods and dark brown woolen capes.

Tom angrily jammed the knitted cap into his pocket and slammed Da's cap on his head. We laughed together when the combination of his hot temper and his embarrassment over the under drawers. The steamy kitchen forced Tom to shed Da's cap and his new coat seconds later. How long would he keep the underwear on, we wondered silently?

Ellen and I were given matching green calico print dresses, white cotton neck cloths and aprons. I had never owned so many layers of underclothes! I now owned a linen chemise, petticoat and drawers. The drawers were strange, but promised to keep my legs warm when my skirts were blown about. I didn't remember ever being so warm and cozy before that day.

While I was twirling around the room, the back door flew open as three large men boisterously entered. They were laughing as they stomped and shook off snow. Holy Mother of

God, it's thankful I was that we were all finally warm and dressed!

Mr. Miles[13] welcomed us in a fatherly manner. He was full of energy like Da had been back home. It was a fond memory for Da never seemed to have his old energy after coming to this new country. Ma said it pained his heart to leave the ould sod.

Mary's green eyes sparkled as Eugene, the only Miles' son, greeted us warmly with a wink to Mary. Did this mean he was her friend? He was taller than she by the length of my arm. His wavy damp brown hair flowed about his shoulders. Mary had later told us he earned good money as a clerk at a hardware store down on Main Street.

Tom cornered Richard Courtney, who worked for Mr. Miles, to discover what was on the roll of paper he carried. Tom's red hair contrasted with Richard's sandy hair as they bent over the sketch of the house Mr. Miles was building. They were about equally tall even though Tom was only twelve. Richard, however, had the broad shoulders of a 21-year-old. He seemed to laugh with every breath. Ellen and I giggled,

---

[13] Jonas M. Miles was listed as a carpenter in the 1850 Census. He served on the Worcester Common Council, was its president and an Alderman in 1850-1. Richard Courtney, 21, was listed as a carpenter and was probably Mr. Miles' apprentice or assistant boarding with the family. The City Directory listed Eugene Miles as a clerk at Calvin Foster & Company at 222 Main Street.

too, when we noticed he frequently caught Mary's eye. It is too bad no one realized how he would later break her heart.

Mary had put Ellen and me to work finishing supper for the Miles' family so we wouldn't embarrass her by staring at these handsome men. We weren't allowed to eat in the big room with the polished table. It dinna matter for we all once again ate as the McLoughlin family around the kitchen table. We savored every bite of cheese and baked apples until Mary broke the cozy spell.

"'Tis a sad thing we canna live together. Remember Ma said, 'the Blessed Lord would never close one gate without opening another. 'Tis up to each of ye to be alert for the right opportunity here in America. Keep your eyes open and never fear what may lie ahead.'"

Suddenly, Richard spoke softly from the doorway, "Henry David Thoreau wrote almost the same thing after living alone on Walden Pond. He wrote, 'Nothing is so much to be feared as fear.'[14] Keep that thought in your hearts as you face the new year and your new lives here in Worcester."

After supper we rode the omnibus through a light snowfall across town to the Orphans' Home. [15] As we pulled up in front of a large white two-and-a-half story house on Pine

---

[14] Thoreau wrote this quotation in his journal 7 September 1851 and it was published in *Walden Pond* in 1855.

[15] The weather for this day in history was not confirmed.

Street, Mother Miles told us, "During the beginning of our nation, Worcester's great patriot publisher Isaiah Thomas lived in this house. He smuggled his printing press out of Boston on the eve of the Revolution and was able to print the first reports of the Battles of Lexington and Concord in his paper, *The Massachusetts Spy*, to inform the rest of the colonies of the first shots fired in the war. Twenty years ago, this house was moved across the city about as far as we traveled this evening, children. We have Sheriff Lincoln to thank for giving the house to the Children's Friend Society." [16]

First Children's Friend Society Orphans' Home on Pine Street.
From collections of the Worcester Historical Museum.

[16] Isaiah Thomas' first house had been moved across the Worcester from its location at High and Pleasant Streets behind Nobility Hill on Main Street to Pine Street (known as Shrewsbury Street today). His smuggled printing press still resides at the American Antiquarian Society in Worcester in 2012.

Tom wanted to hear more about the war against the British tyrants, but we were shiverin' and ready to find a warm hearth. Although I vaguely remembered the British landlords upsetting Ma and Da, I didn't want a history lesson. I wanted to stay with Mary. I had thought we would be living with her. Mary kept her arm tightly around me as I hesitantly walked towards the opening door.

I looked up to see the smiling faces of the matron, Miss White, and her assistant, Miss Gleason, backlit by the warm hearth flames and candle glow. The room was crowded with several other children about my age or younger. Tom seemed to be the oldest boy in the room and boldly warmed his hands by the fire after meeting the women.

Staples' *Worcester Children's Friend .Society*, 1849-1884.

Over a cuppa tea and spicy gingerbread Miss White informed us, "Tom and Ellen will be placed as indentured servants in the nearby town of Shrewsbury.[17] Tom, you'll enjoy working on Mr. Knowlton's farm. Ellen, Widow Noyes is in great need of your help. Her husband recently passed away and her sons, Calvin and Sandford, have inherited the homestead. It's a large family that includes Mrs. Noyes' aging parents."

Tom beamed at the gate that had opened before him. He would once more be able to run free in the open fields instead of the dirty, crowded city. He was not afraid of hard work as long as he could breathe deeply and work with his hands.

"Glory be to God," Ellen whispered with a squeeze to my hand. Tears seeped from my eyes. She was pleased she would be near Tom. Mary had warned her she would be bound out because she was twelve-years-old. The Orphans' Home could not afford to care for children old enough to work and learn a trade. They must promise to work for room and board until they turn eighteen.

Mother Miles reminded them both, "Your kind masters have opened their homes to you out of Christian charity. You

---

[17] The minutes of the 26 January 1850 Children's Friend Society meeting, which may have included Tom and Ellen's indenture records, have been cut out of the ledger at the American Antiquarian Society. A Tom and Ellen Lochlin are listed in the 1850 Shrewsbury Census as living with the families mentioned. See Chapter 1 footnote regarding name changes in U. S. Census records.

will be allowed to attend the village school and the Congregational Church to learn to be good Americans."

"Holy Mother of God!" gasped Ellen. "Is there no Catholic priest?" Mary quickly grabbed her hand to warn her not to complain.

From that moment on my life seemed as turbulent as our storm tossed ship on the vast ocean. My sickness, however, was of my heart. First Ma and Da were gone, then Mary, and now Tom and Ellen were leaving me in this strange place. Ma would be upset if we could not attend mass. Mary had said Father Gibson was kind and understanding over at St. John's, but at the time I did not know I would seldom be allowed to attend mass with her.

The stress of the day captured my thoughts and my eyes drooped. Mary and Mother Miles prepared to leave, but I was hardly aware of the conversation.

That first night I had to sleep across the foot of the bed of the other eight-year-old girls-- Mary Noland, Lucy Parkhurst and Sarah Mixter. My first thought was I would never be cold or hungry again as I snuggled beneath the heavy quilt. Sadly, the girls were not pleased to make space for me and I woke finding my feet numb with cold where the quilt had been pulled away to warm my bedmates. I soon discovered I only had to put up with this discomfort for one night. The following day Ellen signed her indenture and left so I could share a less crowded bed with the two oldest girls.

Mary Jackson smiled and said, "Cindy and I look forward to your body heat, Liza. The winter winds easily find their way into our second floor bedroom." Her words warmed me and made me feel welcome for I had already experienced the cold.

Tom had shared a bed with Joey Williams. Morning found the boys punching each other even before breakfast. We had discovered Joey's anger was like a Lucifer match. Even though he was the oldest boy in the home, he had not been bound out. Cynthia warned me that he easily found trouble--and was always angry with his lot in life.

Personally, I liked the way his black hair flopped forward over his eyes. Joey reminded me of a big puppy. I vowed to make friends with him even though Tom had given him a black eye as a farewell present.

My days at the Orphans' Home fell into a daily routine of meals, housework and schooling. The oldest girls, Mary and Cynthia helped with the two-year-olds, Tommy and Charlie. In fact, Mary was Tommy's sister. I was the nineteenth member of this large "family." [18] To help me settle in, I was put to work peelin' taters and the like to help Miss Jane[19] prepare the

---

[18]The 1850 Census listed all the children introduced except Joseph Williams. Their individual stories could sometimes be followed in the Minutes and Annual Reports of the Society.

[19] Jane Brown, age 25, was the cook at the Orphans' Home, according to the 1850 Census.

meals whenever I wasn't at lessons. I was also expected to darn socks and mend clothes in the evening to practice my homemaking skills while Miss White or Miss Gleason read aloud.

Lessons were my favorite time of day. Miss White or Miss Gleason would gather us in the parlor with our slates to learn our A B Cs and numbers. I delighted at showing Mary my new skills whenever she came to visit. Miss Gleason called me "a sponge".

We also learned to embroider and sew. Everyone was impressed by how quickly I could sew on a button. They had no idea what my life had been like in New York City.

Although I was alone in a house of strangers, it was much more peaceful and the food was more filling than at the Delancy's tenement. Merchants, mechanics, grocers, ministers, farmers, doctors and others supplied the articles necessary to run the Orphans' Home. Church and temperance groups contributed money, books and clothing to meet the needs of our large "family".

Even though I'm a girl, Joey and I eventually became friends. Miss Gleason had made him my reading tutor to help us both become better readers. I surprised them all and soon was helping Joey more than he helped me. I loved to read. I wanted to know more and move onto the next page.

One day, I found a copy of Jewett's *The Youth's Temperance Lecturer* left by Abby Rawson and Emily

Loveland. Their mothers belong to the Ladies' Washingtonian Sewing Circle of Worcester, which sometimes made clothes for us.[20]

The Drunkard at home.

Jewett's *The Youth's Temperance Lecturer* (1841), page 20.
Courtesy, American Antiquarian Society.

I cried when I saw some pictures of drunken husband's beating their wives and children. I vowed never to show Joey this book. Once when I was missing Ma and Da, he said he only missed his ma. His sad story of how his father beat his

---

[20] The Ladies' Washingtonian Sewing Circle of Worcester, founded in 1843 as part of the ladies' temperance group, was dedicated to suppress and diminish the use of intoxicating beverages in their community. The goods they made and sold provided money to support their cause. Abby's mother, Mrs. Abigail Rawson, was the first president as well as one of the Children's Friend Society Board of Managers. Mrs. Loveland, Emily's mother was also a member.

mother to death while in a drunken rage had shocked me out of my selfish loneliness. Joey had also been his father's target. He thought that if he hadn't been hiding that night, his mother might still be alive. Then he would not be at the Orphan's Home. No wonder he was such an angry lad.

I frequently was lonely, but not angry. Miss Gleason taught me to read the *Bible*. One of the first passages I read was John 14:18, "I will not leave you comfortless: I will come to you." So I waited....

In the early fall a soft-spoken young lady of eighteen years and her younger brother came to visit late one morning.[21]

[21] Sarah Folger Earle (1831-1921) was 1st Assistant Principal at the Ash Street Secondary School and would graduate from Framingham Normal School in 1855. Her 15-year-old brother, Pliny (1835-1892), was a mute and may have had a disfigured face, according to family historian Albert Southwick. Sarah and Pliny Earle's help at Orphans' Home is undocumented although their Aunt Ann Earle was the second directress of the Children's Friend Society. Their father, John Milton Earle (1794-1874) served as representative to Massachusetts General Court from 1844-1846 and 1850-1852. An early abolitionist and Free Soiler, he helped make Worcester

I learned that Sarah Earle's father owned *The Worcester Spy* and their family were abolitionists.[22] She wanted to help us, too. She and Miss Gleason were friends. As the assistant principal at the new school on Ash Street, she was interested in our schooling. Unlike her pupils, we never went to the city's schools until we were placed out like Tom and Ellen.

Instantly, I fell in love with Miss Earle's calm demeanor, Quaker[23] straw bonnet and simple light gray dress. Miss Earle gathered us around her in the schoolroom saying, "I thought you would enjoy a Graham cracker[24] while I read today's story."

Tall, gangly Pliny Earle passed out the crackers, but

County a stronghold of conscious and determined political opposition to slavery. The weather when they arrived was not documented.

[22] Abolitionists were people who believed all slavery should end immediately. They were also referred to as anti-slavery people who varied in their beliefs of how quickly slavery should end.

[23] Quakers are a religious group who believe in non-violence and speaking out, whether male or female, when moved by their inner light or soul. This group is also known as the Society of Friends and dressed plainly at the time.

[24] The Graham cracker or dyspepsia cracker was part of Sylvester Graham's new diet reform. It encouraged a strict diet of whole grains, fresh fruits, vegetables and nuts in three daily meals six hours apart with no snacking in between. In addition he prescribed fresh air, cold water bathing every day, and loose fitting clothes.

spoke not a word. At the time it was very strange until I learned he was mute and could not speak. After the story about a black boy named Frederick Douglass, who had taught himself how to read and escaped slavery, Pliny took Joey and the older boys outside to play ball.

As I followed them Miss Jane firmly demanded, "Liza, stay here! You'll help me serve tea to the ladies."

Dejectedly, I turned and found the tea tray thrust into my hands that itched to hold a ball.

"My mother has been asked to open the Woman's Rights Convention this October," Miss Earle was saying as I entered with the honey cakes Miss Jane had baked especially for the Earles who would eat no product made with slave labor, like sugar.

Sitting quietly in the corner near the open window to catch the breeze, I had wondered why these ladies would be interested in such a meeting. They seemed so happy to me. I thought all was right with them compared to my life.

I was feeling I would have liked to demand the right to go play outside with the boys instead of serving tea. It was quite tiresome to be quiet and ladylike.

"OOF!"

"No, Joey!"

"Come on!"

"Pft-t-t-t!"

Hearing the noise, Miss White leapt to her feet disturbing my eavesdropping. We all quickly followed her out back. Pliny lay sprawled in the muddy garden where we learned Joey had hit him forcefully with the ball. The first row of carrots was partially uprooted and the first bean plant broken atop his head.

Without a word Pliny rose to his full height, brushed off the mud and slowly walked up to Joey. He stood directly before him and the boys locked eyes.

We were all shocked to hear Joey softly say, "Sorry, Pliny." None was privy to the silent message that passed between them.

"You could learn a thing or two from this Quaker gentleman, Joey. Thank the good Lord for your voice. Start putting it to good use instead of this physical violence," Miss White admonished as she hauled him away to be punished.

As prim Miss Earle and dirty, but proud, Pliny headed for their home across the Common, I had wondered what their home was like....

Nobility Hill, Main Street, Worcester.
Sandrof's *Massachusetts Towns*.

FRIENDS

On Nobility Hill across   September 4, 1850[25]

from the Common on Main Street

Pliny and Sarah arrived home feeling they had helped enlighten the poor orphans to the plight of enslaved children, even less fortunate than themselves. Pliny, in his filthy condition and frustration over not being able to communicate with the bully, was not as pleased as his sister.

---

[25] The September time frame for Chapters 4-7 is the author's invention. The Call to the first National Woman's Rights Convention was issued 30 May 1850 so the townsfolk would have been discussing the upcoming event throughout the summer and fall. Jenny Lind performed September 11 and 13 in New York City and then toured to Boston and Providence, Rhode Island the first week in October. Her concerts were a hot topic of conversation that fall.

"Thankfully, Nancy finished the laundry yesterday; quickly change out of those dirty clothes," Sarah ordered. "Thee look like a willing participant in a fight, but I am so proud of the way thee showed that errant boy his behavior was unacceptable. One need not physically fight back to be the victor."

Pliny grinned his thanks and ran upstairs. He really didn't need his sister's advice any longer, but enjoyed being home from school in Providence, Rhode Island.

Mrs. Sarah Hussey Earle.
Worcester Women's History Project.
< www.wwhp.org>.

Sarah removed her straw hat, slowly peeled off her gloves and headed for the kitchen in search of her mother. Mrs. Earle was supervising dinner preparations with Lizzie and Cate, her older daughters, along with Cynthia Gardner, the 20-year-old free black woman who helped the family. It was almost two o'clock and Mr. Earle would soon be home from the newspaper office.

Bursting with news, Sarah entered the kitchen. "Mother, Miss White and Miss Gleason were very interested to learn of the Call to the National Woman's Rights Convention. They send their best wishes to thee as the opening speaker.[26] Miss White, however, is concerned our new emphasis on woman's rights may detract from support for the Orphan's Home and cause too much commotion."

"Sarah, thou knowest how many of our anti-slavery friends feel the very same way. I fear these concerns may cause only a small number to gather to discuss the rightful adjustment to woman's rights, duties and relations. Many choose not to see that giving women an equal voice is a way to help solve other problems in our society!"

---

[26] Mrs. Sarah Hussey Earle (1799-1858) opened the convention on 23 October 1850. She was the first president of the Worcester Anti-Slavery Society Sewing Circle in 1841. Elizabeth, Martha and Sarah F. Earle are all known to have attended the first National Woman's Rights Convention although Sarah F. did not sign in as a voting member of the convention. Family nicknames were suggested by family letters, found at the American Antiquarian Society.

"Personally, mother, I think any discussion will bring light to the dark corners of the troubles of our times. Miss Gleason promises to attend. We feel there will be an opportunity to call for equal pay for equal work. I realize I am new to my teaching position, but so is Mr. Starr, who is earning five times my pay at the high school!"[27]

"How did the orphans like the Graham crackers I made?" interrupted Lizzie.

"I heard no complaints and many words of gratitude--especially from Liza McLoughlin. That orphan's curiosity is unquenchable. I wish my students were all such eager scholars. It is a shame she cannot attend the public schools, but Louisa Gleason tells me she is already in the second reader. Louisa's working on her recitation to eliminate that thick Irish accent. Liza tells me she'd like to be a teacher like me someday. I certainly hope teachers' pay will be equal by then," Sarah commented as she carried a bowl of quince sauce to the table.

---

[27] Sarah F. Earle earned $170 as 1st Assistant Principal at the Ash Street Secondary School according to the Report of the School Committee in 1850 Worcester Report. Students admitted to the Secondary Schools had to be able to read fluently in Primary School reading books, to spell words in those books, be familiar with the stops, abbreviations, number, figures, the multiplication table, and arithmetic and geography prescribed by those schools. The school year of forty-four weeks was divided into three terms, 9 A.M. to 4 P.M. with an hour for lunch and two fifteen minute recesses. Minimum age to begin Primary School was four. There was a high school entrance exam after passing the Grammar School level (considered a secondary level).

Mr. Earle, Pliny, Martha and Fanny were already seated at the dining room table. The family joined hands and bowed their heads for a moment of silent thanksgiving.

"Amen," whispered Mrs. Earle and passed the bread.

As always, Mr. Earle began the dinner conversation. "My, Pliny, thee look much neater after your trip to the barber. What news did thee hear at Clough's?"

Jenny Lind's New York Concert. Wikipedia. <en.wikipedia.org>.

1850 daguerreotype of Jenny Lind. Wikipedia. <en.wikipedia.org>.

Gracefully moving his hands, Pliny signed that Stephen Salisbury[28] had recently returned from hearing Jenny Lind sing. Stephen had shown everyone Ms. Lind's concert souvenir

---

[28] Fifteen-year-old Stephen Salisbury III was the son of one of the most influential industrialists in town.

picture. Pliny's silly grin showed he would have liked to hear the "Swedish Nightingale", too. All of his sisters from 10-year-old Fanny to 26-year-old Lizzie eagerly expressed their interest as well. There had been so much publicity about this talented Swedish woman employed by P. T. Barnum.[29]

"Now children, thee know it is more important to spend thy money and energies on more important things," Mrs. Earle remanded quietly. "The Anti-Slavery Bazaar is fast approaching. We must ensure good sales now that this horrible new Fugitive Slave Law[30] has taken effect."

Pliny's hands went into action, "Mr. Clough said there are fugitive slaves hiding in town. Is this true, Father?"

"I imagine so, Pliny. Everyone knows the Fosters often have guests stop at their Liberty Farm enroute to Canada. Slave catchers now have the legal right to enlist the help of the town police to capture what they refer to as their property. Of course, they will have trouble finding any officer who will help

---

[29] Phineas T. Barnum operated a museum in New York City. He hired Swedish soprano Jenny Lind in an effort to offer more cultured entertainment to average Americans. Her debut at Castle Garden in New York on 11 September 1850 drew an audience of 5,000. Tickets were in great demand as she went on tour to Boston and other cities.

[30] The new harsh law required the return of runaway slaves because they were considered property like a runaway workhorse. Anyone assisting a fugitive slave could be fined $1000 or jailed up to 6 months beginning in September 1850.

them here in Worcester. The free blacks in town also do what they can to assist their enslaved brothers and sisters."

"How could Senator Daniel Webster agree to such a horrendous compromise just to enable California to become a free state?" asked Martha. "I thought he had stronger principles. There can be NO compromise between right and wrong!"

Mrs. Earle answered, "I think he understands most people who sympathize with the plight of the enslaved will ignore the new law, Martha. We may not agree, but our democracy operates on a system of compromises. How else could it work when there are so many different needs and interests in our country? The northern textile manufacturers must have their southern cotton--the cheaper the better. In the long run, it is far more important to gain the additional free votes in the House and Senate. The southern slave votes will soon be out-numbered by the free northern states and the newer states out west.[31] It's just a matter of time."

---

[31] Each state has an equal two votes in Senate law and decision-making. With the addition of California in 1850, the southern states were gradually losing their majority to protect their peculiar institution of slavery against the free states' votes. Even though about 25% the southerners owned slaves, the Constitution gave 60% more votes in the House of Representatives to the southern states under the three-fifths rule for counting the enslaved population.

Mr. Earle retorted, "President Fillmore[32] will not be up to the task of keeping the new compromise in effect. President Taylor's[33] unexpected death in July should prove how executive power is peacefully transferred to the vice president. It is ironic that the hero of Buena Vista did not live to see that the Mexican War might result in more free soil than slave. He fought to gain access to new land for the cotton plantations, but we Free Soilers expect any new state formed in the Mexican Cession to choose to be free. That is the advantage of popular sovereignty-- free and independent settlers don't want slave labor."

"But Father, what's to stop slave masters from settling and taking control of the new territories even though the climate is not good for growing cotton?" argued Cate. "The new compromise is spreading the debate and even bloodshed into every western territory. This compromise has destroyed the Missouri Compromise."

---

[32] President Millard Fillmore took office on 9 July 1850 following President Taylor's sudden death after only sixteen months in office.

[9] President Zachary Taylor had defeated the Mexicans at Buena Vista at the end of the Mexican War (23 February 1847) fought to settle the border lines with the United States. He was the last president to own slaves while in office and hoped the new south western states would allow slavery.

"Shouldn't we be more concerned about the poor slaves? Their lives are at stake every moment of the day," Fanny reminded everyone.

Sarah could hold her tongue no longer. "I agree, Fanny. I think it is our responsibility to improve people's situations in the here and now. Three-quarters of our family have no right to vote for our lawmakers who do the long term planning. It is up us to make a difference where we can. I'm proud of the excellent work Mother and we girls do in raising money for the Worcester County Anti-Slavery Society. Father's paper keeps the people in town informed and helps them understand the issues. Just this afternoon I had tea with Louisa Gleason at the Orphan's Home. She agrees with Mrs. Stanton--women should have the right to vote. Today, she loaned me her most recent issue of *The Lily*."[34]

"I have wonderful news!" Mrs. Earle announced as everyone returned to eating. "Cousin Lucretia[35] will be staying

---

[34] *The Lily* was a monthly newspaper published by Amelia Bloomer from 1849-1857 first as a forum for women who found themselves silenced in the male controlled temperance movement, then as a voice on all interests to women.

[35] Mrs. Earle and her cousin Lucretia Mott both grew up on the Massachusetts' island of Nantucket. Lucretia was a Quaker reformer who organized the Philadelphia Female Anti-Slavery Society in 1833. When she was denied the right to participate as a member of the American delegation to the 1840 World's Anti-Slavery Convention in London, she and Elizabeth Cady Stanton vowed to do something to improve woman's rights. In 1848 they organized the first Woman's Rights Convention in Seneca Falls, New York. Her husband James Mott was the president of that convention since it would not be acceptable for a woman to hold such a leadership position.

with us during the October convention. It's too bad Cousin James will be unable to leave Philadelphia for this trip. Lucretia writes that Mrs. Stanton also will be unable to attend due to family matters.[36] Regardless of our absent friends who were at the Seneca Falls Convention two years ago, it will be an exciting time. Lucretia has come to agree more strongly that women must take responsibility for changing the wrongs of society by gaining the vote. Sarah, I'm sure thee remembers Lucretia's warning about female teachers' pay. Sadly, things have not improved much since she and James were educators. She may have some suggestions for improving the situation here in Worcester. I'm especially interested in hearing more about the new Female Medical College of Pennsylvania. By her life, Cousin Lucretia reminds us, we must not be slovenly in our efforts."

"Well then, Mother, did thee ever notice Alcott's *Young Woman's Guide* doesn't have a copy of the United States Constitution in it like his *Young Man's Guide*?"

Pliny's hands and shocked expression caught everyone's attention. "Fanny! What are thee doing looking in my book?"

---

[36] Mrs. Elizabeth Cady Stanton was expecting her fourth child. She did not attend any National Woman's Rights Conventions until after the Civil War because of her family responsibilities, but always sent messages from her home in Seneca Falls, New York.

"Pliny, no harm is done," Mrs. Earle interrupted. "It's just as important for girls to be knowledgeable about their government even if they have no voice in it. At the very least they will be raising sons someday. Who knows, perhaps after the Woman's Rights Convention in a few weeks, there will be a greater effort towards universal suffrage in our so-called democracy. Fanny, it is important to honor your brother's privacy even though he has a habit of leaving his books lying around the parlor."

Cynthia silently entered with a huge bowl of fresh raspberries and a pitcher of cream. As the delightful treat was passed around the table Mr. Earle asked, "Cynthia, we've been discussing the possibility of universal suffrage in America. Would thee like to have the right to vote?"

"Oh, Mr. Earle, you know I haven't enough schoolin' to make such important decisions. Of course, if my vote could help end slavery, I might study up on the matter."

As the meal ended Lizzie requested, "Mother, may Sarah read from *The Lily* while we sew tonight?"

Sarah already knew her first selection would be the lyrics to Jenny Lind's "Bird Song".

Johns Hopkins Research. <jscholarship.library.jhu.edu>.

When I would play my song
 You used to sing along.
I always seem to forget
 How fragile are the very strong.
I'm sorry I can't steal you
I'm sorry I can't stay
 So I put band-aids on your knees
 And watch you fly away

I'm sending you away tonight
 I'll put you on a bird's strong wing
 I'm saving you the best way I know how
 I hope again one day to hear you sing

You know we're not so far away
 Get on a boat, get on a train
 And if you ever think you're drowning
 I'll try to slow the rain
 In two years or so
 Drop me a line
 Write me a letter
  I hope to find you're doing better, better than
today, better everyday

I'm sending you away tonight
 I'll put you on a bird's strong wing
 I'm saving you the best way I know how
 I hope again one day to hear you sing
 I'm saving you the only way that I know how
 I hope again one day to hear you sing
 I hope again one day to see you bring your
smile back around again

We hold these truths to be self-evident, that all men are created equal,
that they are endowed y their Creator with certain unalienable Rights,
that among these are Life, Liberty and the pursuit of Happiness.
Declaration of Independence

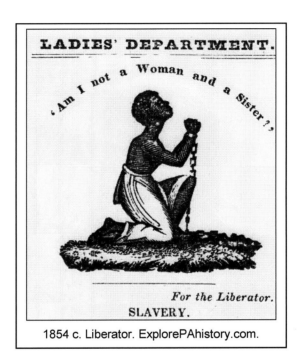

1854 c. Liberator. ExplorePAhistory.com.

HAPPY BIRTHDAY!

While cramped almost under the railcar seat, I tried to figure out how I had come to this moment in my life. I determined most of my discontent began when I turned nine and my responsibilities at the Orphans' Home increased. But for every new twist along my path, I met new friends and saw possible gates to open along the way.

Orphans' Home   September 8, 1850

Pine Street, Worcester

     Following church services at the Salem Street Church, we gathered around the large table for Sunday dinner. Even though it was the usual baked beans, brown bread and Indian pudding for dessert, I could hardly contain my excitement on this, my birthday.[37] I didn't even care that Miss White would not let me attend mass at Saint John's with Mary. By now I realized I had no choice. The Orphans' Home was my home and I had to follow the rules. According to Miss White, I must forget my old papist ways and accept the Protestant God. Tom complained she was as bad as the English Prods.[38]

     However, even Ma would have agreed with the minister. I was determined to follow the words of today's sermon, "Whatsoever thy hand findeth to do, do it with thy might." I decided to make the best of every situation that came my way.

     Miss Gleason, as usual, smoothed my way. "Liza, you have blossomed into a young girl of letters during the ten months you have been with us. This journal is my gift for you to write in every day. It is especially for Sundays when I hope you will reflect on God's blessings on you and how you have measured up to Christian standards."

---

[37] Eliza McLoughlin's exact birth date is undocumented.

[38] English Protestants who were not tolerant of Irish Catholics.

I beamed my gratitude and Miss White quickly joined in. "Here is your very own new quill pen and a bottle of ink to transfer your thoughts into your journal, Liza." Then she surprised me even further by announcing, "Liza, you will join the older girls helping Nancy Powers with the laundry beginning this week.[39] I'm pleased with your accomplished sewing, but you have other housekeeping skills to learn. We are so blessed that Mr. and Mrs. Edward Earle pay Mrs. Powers to do our laundry and help train our growing family.[40]

These gifts truly set me on a new adventure. I delighted in recording new discoveries and wise quotations in my journal and dutifully counted my blessings and shortcomings. The opening words would be from today's sermon.

That evening I learned how to sort clothes by color and type of material. I really had never thought much about laundry, except for the dirty diapers I sometimes had to rinse out, soak and boil in the back yard. Miss Jane said they just couldn't wait for washday.

---

[39] Nancy Rich Powers was a laundress according to the 1850 City Directory. We do not know if she actually worked for the Earles or did laundry at her home. Many laundresses did the work at the home of their employer.

[40] Mr. and Mrs. Edward Earle, Sarah and Pliny's aunt and uncle, were avid supporters of the Children's Friend Society. They may have paid to have Orphans' Home laundry done or perhaps the Orphans' Home did its own laundry.

The following morning after our usual breakfast porridge, I joined the older girls in lugging the sorted laundry three blocks to Nancy Power's home on Summer Street. Joey grudgingly helped, for he considered this woman's work. However, he was always happy to be free from Miss White's iron will while escorting us, no matter how brief the moment. As we walked he told scary stories about the huge Insane Asylum looming on our right and about girls drowning in the canal just the other side of Summer Street. Of course, I believed him at the time since I had never walked this way before. Our usual walk to church bore off to the left.

I felt heat as we opened the gate in the high wooden fence between two nearly identical two story houses. We found two bubbling caldrons of boiling water steaming in the back yard tended by a colored girl about my age with long braids artfully arranged on her head.

"Hiya, Becca!" Mary and Cindy called out as they grabbed some of the dirty clothes and headed directly to different tubs of sudsy water.

I stood there stupidly, not knowing what to do. Joey was no help as he quickly disappeared after dropping his bundles in a heap on the ground.

"I'm Becca White.[41] Who you be?"

"Eliza McLoughlin," I shyly whispered for I had never before spoken to a person of color. My curiosity quickly overcame my shyness as two almond shaped eyes returned my stare under curly black bangs. Her skin was a tawny golden brown, so different from my pale freckled cheeks. I remember thinking my skin would be all brown, too, if all those freckles ever connected.

Becca showed me how to take my load of colored clothes to a special tub of lukewarm water. "Auntie Nancy uses beef gall to hold the colors fast. She be out soon to meet you and boss us 'round."

"Why did the white clothes go into those kettles?" I asked, my curiosity rising.

---

[41] Becca was Clara Rebecca White living in one of Grandpa Peter Rich's properties at the corner of Summer Street and Washington Square. According to the 1850 Census, she was 11 and did not attend school.

"They have lye in 'em and the sheets take up too much room to put in one pot. Come now, time to scrub spots. You sure is curious! Auntie sez the mouth can flap long as the hands is busy."

Just then a tall ebony skinned woman with a red and white striped scarf tied around her head and a white apron entered the yard. Everyone greeted her warmly. "And who's this, Becca?" she asked us a rich deep voice.

"Auntie, this is Liza. She be here to learn 'bout doin' laundry."

"Well, we're always pleased to see more help, Liza. Time's a wastin' ladies. We'll set Mary's load a boilin' and let's get those spots scrubbed. Then you can help wring out, Liza, after I fish out the clean hot clothes and give 'em a good rinse," Auntie said and grabbed a long broomstick with a forked end.

My arms felt like lead by the time we finished one load. Becca laughed, "Come on, Liza, now we add bluing and dip them in starch before we finally hang 'em out to dry. Keep movin' so yer arms don't know they's tired."

The work was hot and wet, but many hands under Auntie Nancy's direction sped along the process. Becca never stopped chattering away. She told tales of her granddaddy and uncle working for the rich folk in town, like the Salisburys. And how her family helped hide fugitive slaves on the Underground Railroad. I had never heard of this railroad underground.

"Oh, Liza, that mean secret, not real tunnels under dirt," Becca giggled when I said my train ride to Worcester was above ground. [42]

As we dragged ourselves home, I could see why Mary and Cindy had been happy to have my help. Even though the work was exhausting, I think we all savored the change of routine from caring for the little ones. I had hardly even missed my lessons that first day. There had been so much to learn about doing laundry.

"Wait until ironing day, Liza!" teased Cindy. "Be glad 'tis fall. This is the most pleasant season for doin' laundry chores.

---

[42] The Underground Railroad was an arrangement to help slaves escape into Canada or another place of safety by passing slaves along a series of safe hiding places by conductors who knew the next safe stop.

Summer and winter are no joy. Tomorrow, Mrs. Clough will put us to work while Mrs. Powers does another family's wash. Poor Becca seldom has a change."

"Doesn't she go to school?"

"Only when she was too little to help her mother with the laundry. But her cousins do. One of them was the first colored gal who passed the entrance exam for the Classical and English High School four years ago. Mrs. Clough[43] is always tellin' us how important book larnin' is. You'll love her, Liza, since yer book smart, too," laughed Mary.

---

[43] According to the 1850 Census Francis A. Clough, 33, and Harriet B. Clough, 30, had four children attending school: Charles, 10, Frances, 6, Frederick, 5, and Anna, 4, while Martina, 3, and Theodore, 1, stayed home. Their last daughter, Jennie Clough (1857-1928), had not yet been born. She became the first woman of color to graduate from Worcester High School in 1875 and Worcester Normal School in 1878. Picture below from the Worcester State University website. Harriet and Nancy Powers were both daughters of Peter Rich. Mr. Clough was the first black to serve on a jury in Massachusetts. Benjamin Clough, Francis' brother, was first black postman in Worcester.

Jennie Cora Clough

Flat Iron. Object Lessons.
<www.objectlessons.org>.

I could hardly drag myself out of bed the next day, but my eagerness to meet Mrs. Clough pulled me into action and we headed back to Summer Street.[44] Mary, Cindy and I were allowed to walk without Joey since we had no heavy load to tote today. I had decided to ignore his scary tall tales anyway.

"Bye, Daddy," a crowd of little children were calling as a short brown skinned man with broad shoulders walked towards us, smiling back over his shoulder at the children. A tall, curly headed boy about my age led three little children off up Summer Street. A short round woman in a green calico

---

[44] 84% of the African-Americans in Worcester lived in properties owned by Peter Rich. Most were in the Summer Street area by 1848 according to Dr. Thomas Doughton.

headscarf stood in the doorway holding a baby boy while a little girl peeked from behind her mother's skirts.

"Mornin' to you ladies," greeted Mrs. Clough. "And you must be Liza. Becca told me you'd be helpin' the girls today. Now that the little ones are off to school, we must get to work. Cindy, stoke up that fire and show Liza where to find more wood to heat the irons. Mary, I'd like you to watch Martina and Teddy today."

We built up the fire to heat the four flat irons and two fluting irons for ruffles. Cindy set up two boards across the backs of a couple chairs. After covering each with a thin blanket, she began ironing skirts. Mrs. Clough assigned me to deliver hot irons from the stove whenever she or Cindy called for a new one. She worked on the more difficult articles of clothing.

Mrs. Clough and her sister Nancy divided the laundry work so she could stay home with her little ones. Sometimes Becca would watch them while Mrs. Clough did ironing with Nancy at the home of her employers.

"Mr. Clough prefers I stay at home while the children are little," she told me. "He makes a good living as a barber at his shop over on the first floor of the City Hall."

Worcester City Hall.
Preservation Worcester. <www.preservationworcester.org>.

The three of us were invited to share dinner with Mr. and Mrs. Clough, their six children and two boarders. Of course we were expected to help bring the meal to the table. It was not difficult since our mouths had been watering all morning as the aroma of slow cooking pork filled the air. That week I began to appreciate the old saying, "Many hands make light work." I also noticed that a housewife needed to be very organized if she added any new moneymaking task to those she already had caring for her family.

What a treat to eat dinner with a REAL family. Mr. Clough said grace in a low baritone voice before telling his wife, and the other eager ears gathered around the table, the news in town.

"Mother, young Salisbury was in for a haircut today braggin' that he heard Jenny Lind sing in Boston. He entertained the waiting customers by passing around her picture and carrying on about her lovely voice."

"Imagine having money to spend on such frivolous entertainment!" commented Mrs. Clough. "I did, however, read in the paper that Miss Lind donated some of her earnings to the Colored Orphans' Asylum and other needy groups in New York City."

But everyone wanted to hear more about Barnum's newest sensation. I briefly considered a career on stage. Thoughts of my off key hymn singing just last Sunday quickly squashed that plan.

As if he was reading our thoughts, Mr. Clough continued, "Beware of jealousy...the green-eyed monster.[45] Work hard and you'll be able to do the same types of things. Stephen's granddaddy was a tradesman just like me when he came to Worcester almost a hundred years ago to open his hardware shop. My trade, too, has steadily grown in the fifteen years I've been here."

I was only listening with half an ear as I busily ate a huge helping of fresh beets, applesauce, pulled pork and potatoes until I caught Mrs. Clough saying...

"... a discussion of woman's rights at Brinley Hall. Nancy said Mrs. Earle will open the convention. I suppose all of the men are laughing at the prospect. Several of the women from church feel we must attend to remind others, simply by our presence, that our enslaved sisters are American women, too. I was pleased to read Mrs. Stowell's letter to the editor in

---

[45] "Jealousy ... a green eyed monster" was paraphrased from Shakespeare's *Othello*.

The Liberator promising ladies from abroad 'warm and sympathizing hearts' in Worcester." [46]

"Actually, Mother, I've heard mixed comments about a national gathering of strong-minded women and their male supporters. Most of my customers, even the most liberal, see no reason for such a convention here in town. Some just snort, 'More Garrisonians!'"

"The good news is that Frederick Douglass[47] and Sojourner Truth[48] have sent word they plan to attend, reported Mrs. Clough. "Do you think the deacons[49] might arrange a special meeting with the congregation? I've heard he plans to speak on the Fugitive Slave Law in surrounding towns."

---

[46] *The Liberator* was a monthly newspaper published by William Lloyd Garrison (1805-1879) beginning in 1831 to demand immediate abolition of slavery and an end to racism. Mrs. Stowell's letter to the editor is in the 20 September 1850 issue.

[47] Frederick Douglass (1818-1895) was an educated former slave who gave anti-slavery lectures and published the *North Star*. In 1848 he attended the first Woman's Rights Convention in Seneca Falls, New York.

[48] Sojourner Truth (c.1779-1883) was born into slavery in New York as Isabella. She changed her name when she took to the road as an independent preacher.

Ten-year-old Charlie muttered, "I'd rather hear Mr. Douglass speak about how he became a free man. What a circus such a convention of women would be! It would be better to hear that Lind lady sing." The two boarders both laughed, nodding their heads and I actually agreed with Charlie, but kept my own counsel.

"Hush with that kind of talk Charles. Your mother works as hard, if not harder, raising you to be a man and managing our home while I work to put food on the table and a roof over your head, young man. Count your blessings that you are free and able to receive a good education, unlike our poor brethren enslaved in the south."

"May our daughters be as corner pillars of thy palace," reprimanded Mrs. Clough.[50]

The conversation moved on to other topics as everyone finished. We girls helped clear the table. The men had to

---

[49] The Cloughs were active members of the African Methodist Episcopal Zion Church founded in 1846 in the basement of a home on Summer Street.

[50] Psalm 144:12 in *Bible*.

return to their shop and we had to finish the ironing. I traded jobs with Mary watching the four children not put down for naps. I pretended I was their teacher while Charlie worked on his ciphering. He told me his father expected him to help run the shop. Overhearing our conversation, little Anna said, "I'm going to be a hairdresser in daddy's shop, too, Liza. Let me fix your braids."[51]

"Will people let you do that? Don't they look down on colored folk here in Worcester?"

"My granddaddy owns most of the houses in the neighborhood. He inherited his first property from a colored Patriot who fought for our country's independence," answered Charlie, "side by side with the white Patriots. That's why our house is nicer than those shanties you Irish live in. Guess it's different down south, but here in Worcester, black folk earn their way. Father's a respected man here and cuts most of the town leaders' hair."

---

[51] Anna Clough did grow up to be a hairdresser in Worcester.

I wondered why Charlie didn't like Irish folk. Didn't he know I lived at the Orphans' Home?

From that day, however, I began to consider the possibility of working in a shop like Anna wanted to do as a hairdresser. After all, some women made hats and some were dressmakers. It would be important for them to learn how to cipher, too. I would have to ask Miss Gleason if I might learn to cipher soon.

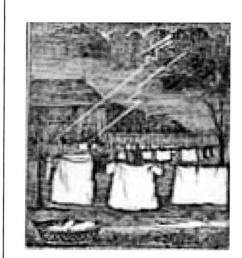

Washing Day.
Courtesy, American Antiquarian Society.

'Tis a foolish self-deceiving,
*   By such tricks to hope for gain;*
All that's ever got by thieving,
*   Turns to sorrow, shame, and pain.*

From "The Thief" in Rev. Isaac Watts'
Divine and Moral Songs for Children

Blackstone Canal. Old Sturbridge Village. <www.osv.org>.

THE FUGITIVE

Memories of the good times at the Orphans' Home made me want to rise up from my hiding place and run back to Mother Miles. I had found solace in the love and routine I found there. However, it took me very little time to realize that while I enjoyed Becca's company, I did not like doing laundry. I would never choose that gate willingly. Miss Gleason once said teachers often board with families who take care of their laundry, cooking and cleaning so they are free to teach. This path was definitely more to my liking, but did not yet seem within my grasp.

Suddenly I heard loud voices in the back of the railway car and suddenly remembered what had happened to another fugitive from the Orphans' Home.

Worcester, Massachusetts   September 16, 1850

That morning I woke early to help dress the little ones for breakfast. Mary, Cynthia and two of the younger girls were helping Miss Jane in the kitchen this week. It was hoped we would all become skilled in our future domestic roles through this practice. And indeed, I had learned how to cook many things with few complaints from the diners.

I much preferred taking care of the children, who asked questions showing they were as eager as I was to learn new things. Perhaps I could become a schoolteacher. Every day I learned new words and tried to read yet another book. Miss Gleason said I was her keenest pupil. I had become one of the chosen Bible readers every Sunday evening, which is a great honor.

That morning I found both 2-year-olds, Charlie and Tommy, crying in the bed they share. Hugs were not enough to calm them so I could discover what was wrong.

"Joey... Mama's.... locket," wailed Tommy.

"He-e-e hit me," snuffled Charlie.

"Let's get you dressed and we'll find Joey. Why would he do something like this?"

"Liza...he-e-e hurt us," whispered Charlie.

"I want Mommy's picture back!" screamed Tommy.

The three of us tumbled down the stairs to more chaos. Cynthia had just reported a missing blackberry pie, a wedge of cheese and some apples

Tommy's and Charlie's information was added to the growing pool of evidence. Miss White stormed off to find Joey who seemed to be the only one missing in the parlor by this point of the commotion. His bedmates, Jimmy and Persis, claimed he slipped out of bed to use the chamber pot in the middle of the night, but was not in bed when they awoke to do their chore of emptying the pots in the necessary out back.

What had Joey gone and done now?! Last night at supper he'd seemed unusually friendly and happy. I had thought it was on account of Miss White's announcement that she found a farmer in Auburn willing to give Joey a chance for work.

Miss White returned after thoroughly searching the house and yard. Jimmy and Persis were sent to bring Mother Miles and a constable. "Joey Williams has been nothing but trouble since the day the Children's Friend Society took him under their wing," muttered Miss Gleason.

What a morning! Life in my new home was certainly not boring. Before breakfast could be served, there was a knock at the front door just as we started to gather around the table.

Pliny Earle came in expressing with signs and facial expression his apologies for the early hour. He handed Miss White a note.

"Oh my, you lost a gold piece the other day? Are you sure, Pliny? Did anyone find it out back?" she asked everyone.

The question was met with a sea of stunned faces as each of us put two and two together. We all silently spooned up our porridge, afraid to put our thoughts into words for fear of setting the little ones off again.

After breakfast Mr. Curtis delivered some fresh milk from his farm southwest of the city on Upland Street. Miss Jane was bubbling over with the morning's excitement.

"Ya know, Miss Jane, I seen a strange young fellow walking along the canal path on my way into town. Looked to be heading for Providence, mayhap the ocean. Does he have black hair and a checkered coat?" he asked, eager to help.

By now Mother Miles and the constable had arrived. Hearing the farmer's report, they decided to head out along the Blackstone Canal.[52]

Courtesy of Animal Photos.
<farm1.static.flickr>.

---

[52] The Blackstone Canal was built in 1828 along Blackstone River where America's Industrial Revolution began to connect Worcester, Massachusetts to Providence, Rhode Island and the Atlantic Ocean. Competition from the railroad parallel to the canal, droughts and freezing winters brought an end to its usefulness.

I took Charlie and Tommy into the parlor to talk to the two canaries that kind Mrs. Brown had brought us yesterday. We tried to think of good names for them as they sang from their cage. Thankfully, the boys were soon distracted from the lost locket that held their mother's daguerreotype. It was their only memory of her. Jimmy had let his little brother wear it the last few days. I had always wished I had had a picture of Ma and Da, but one cannot wish for what cannot be.

Later that afternoon, Joey was dragged into the room by the constable followed by Mother Miles. Miss Gleason hurriedly led all the children outside to clean up the garden and yard.

About an hour later, Miss White brought Joey outside. Head down and teary eyed, he walked up to Charlie and Tommy Noland. "I'm sorry I took yer ma's locket. Yer lucky to have each other and this memento to remind you of her."

He then came up to each of us to apologize for bullying us in the past and to say good-bye. Mother Miles, Miss White and the constable had decided the State Reform School at Westboro was the only recourse left to them for such an unruly boy. Pliny Earle's stolen gold piece was the last straw in a long chain of petty thievery on Joey's part.[53]

---

[53] Although the theft is fiction, Joseph Williams was sent to the State Reform School at Westboro according to the Board minutes of 29 June 1850 and earlier Joseph Conaldson "proving so perverse + refractory in disposition + so vicious in his habits" had also been sent according to the Board minutes of 26 May 1849.

"When Joey's actions affected people outside of the Home, the consequences must be paid," the constable warned us all.

I was sad to see Joey leave under these circumstances. Even though I somewhat understood his anger and loneliness, he never saw the opportunities the Children's Friend Society tried to provide for each of us nor had he ever tried to forgive his father. That night we all prayed for him.

And now I am the fugitive. I wonder if the Westboro Reformatory takes girls.

Life is real; life is earnest;
*   And the grave is not its goal;*
Dust thou art, to dust returnest,
*   Was not spoken of the soul.*

Not enjoyment and not sorrow,
*   Is our destined end or way,*
But to act, that each to-morrow,
*   Find us farther than to-day."*

William Longfellow's "A Psalm of Life",
McGuffey's *Sixth Eclectic Reader*
quoted in the *Children's Friend Society*
First Annual Report

Excerpt of 1840-1855 Salisbury Mansion
daguerreotype. From collections of the
Worcester Historical Museum.

GATES ACROSS TOWN

*I bet it was Henry Rawson who turned us in this morning! I
had always thought the children who visited us in the
Orphans' Home were my friends. I'd like to think he felt he
was stopping me from making a mistake, but more likely,
he feared what his mother would say since she's on the
Board of Managers.*

What if I was her child or Mrs. Salisbury's? I had often wondered how other Worcester children spent their days.

Worcester, Massachusetts   October 9, 1850

A shy young girl dressed in a frilly pink dress delicately picked at her food while her new step-brother sat politely at the breakfast table in Stephen Salisbury's elegant stone mansion on the lower slope of the hill at the north end of Main Street. Mr. Salisbury and his second wife Nancy had just returned from their brief honeymoon. Mr. Salisbury had come up with a plan to help his children become more acquainted as he prepared to leave his family for the day to care for his banking and business concerns.[54]

Stephen Salisbury II.
Courtesy, Worcester Art Museum.

---

[54] Stephen Salisbury II (1798-1884) lived in the building that is now the American Red Cross in Worcester on Harvard Street with his son Stephen III. Stephen's mother died of consumption when he was 8-years-old (the same age as Eliza McLoughlin was orphaned). Stephen's father married the widow of Captain George Lincoln, Nancy Hoard Lincoln (1820-1852) in October, 1850. Georgianna DeVillers Lincoln (1841-1861) was his new stepdaughter.

"Your Grandmother would like you and Georgianna to deliver a bundle of articles she has sewn for the orphans this afternoon, Stephen. I have a basket of your hand-me-downs to send, as well."

"Yes, father," young Stephen replied with visibly mixed feelings about this errand. It wasn't that he didn't love to visit Grandmother or see the value of helping the orphans, especially since father was a member of the Board of Directors of the Children's Friend Society. He just would not choose Georgianna for a companion on his walk across town on a superb fall day. He felt immediate guilt for he knew it was his duty as an older brother to introduce her to the Salisbury benevolent concerns. There was no choice, but to uphold the family's reputation.[55]

Stephen's grandmother lived in a large old mansion at the bottom of the hill.[56] His grandfather, Stephen Salisbury, had built their house and hardware store when he came to town a few years before the War for Independence.[57] The 200-

---

[55] Stephen Salisbury III (1835-1905) attended Worcester's Classical and English High School on Walnut Street and graduated from Harvard in1856 to continue in his father's footsteps in business and banking. He regularly attended the First Unitarian Church by the Court House. His upbringing led him to donate time and money to many philanthropies, especially the Worcester Art Museum, American Antiquarian Society and Worcester County Music Association.

[57] Grandmother Salisbury, Elizabeth Tuckerman Salisbury (1768-1851), was actually in Boston during the period of this story. She was listed in the Second Annual Report of the Children's Friend Society as donating clothes. Her husband had been a successful merchant from 1772 until his death in

acre Salisbury farm extended from Lincoln Square to beyond Park Avenue.

1848-1855 Salisbury Mansion daguerreotype.
Courtesy, Worcester Art Museum.

Well trained, Stephen showed Georgianna how to wipe her feet on the sheepskin mat in the entry. He immediately darted into the library to the left of the front door to return the borrowed copy of Milton's *Paradise Lost*. His grandmother was so pleased he had finally read it from cover to cover. One of her greatest disappointments was that Stephen and his father did not attend the Calvinist Central Church, but chose to attend the more liberal Unitarian Church.

The children found their grandmother in the drawing rooms just across the hall. She had created these rooms out of the old hardware store portion of the house after her husband passed away. Georgianna beamed at the sight of the pianoforte while Stephen ran his hands over the strings of the

1829. The Salisbury Mansion was moved up the hill on Highland Street in 1929 where it still stands as a museum.

wind harp made of wood with delicate ivory inlay as he had done on every visit since he was a child. Even at fifteen he felt his grandmother expected this ritual before hugging her. Stephen then gently pushed Georgianna forward where she could warily give her new grandmother a slight embrace.

Grandma Salisbury.
Courtesy, Worcester Art Museum.

"Welcome, Georgianna and Stephen. How are your father and his new bride?" Grandmother Salisbury asked from her favorite red mahogany rocker as the children took a seat on the carved sofa.

"They are fine, Grandmother, " Stephen answered more brightly than he felt and quickly changed the subject. "Are you feeling better?"

"Yes, dear. Well enough that I have finished some undergarments for the girls at the Orphans' Home. Your father tells me you have a delivery of your own to make this morning. I am so proud of the benevolence of my men. It is vital we share our good fortune with the less fortunate and now Georgianna can help."

Their grandmother noticed her new granddaughter's inattention. "Would you like to play a song on the pianoforte, my dear?"

"Oh yes, madam," Georgianna gushed. She gracefully arranged herself and played a pretty little piece.

Her small audience clapped appreciatively.

"I would so enjoy hearing more whenever it is possible. You play delightfully, child," her new grandmother encouraged.

Stephen's brain was racing. How could he escape the female chatter? He was not used to having women around since his mother died seven years ago and now his grandmother was brushing him out of the discussion. Suddenly, he had a gallant solution, "Grandmother, perhaps, we could stop by Mr. Rawson's confectionery while we're in the neighborhood. Would you like me to bring you back a special treat?"

"Umm. You know I'm partial to lemon Gibraltars. Has he started making your favorite Turkish Delight candy, yet? You were raving about them when you came back from Boston."

"His son, Henry, is far more interested in trying to make them than Mr. Rawson. I'll stop for your treat anyway and maybe some cachou."

"Why not buy two dozen hard comfits for the children at the Home while you're there? I think your father mentioned there are about twenty children there now. Here's 25 cents."

"Thank you, Grandmother. They'll enjoy the treat. Most of the donations from the merchants and tradesmen go towards the basics needed to nurture their bodies and souls. Sweet treats always elevate my spirits and surely will help theirs."

"Georgianna, why don't you bring my treat when you and your mother come to tea tomorrow? I'll look forward to another song," and gave her a farewell hug.

"Goodbye, Grandmother," Stephen whispered kissing her cheek. She had been his lifeline since his mother passed on and he was concerned for she did not seem well.

Stephen decided it was more proper to walk down Summer Street past the impressive State Hospital for the Insane. "Georgianna, did you know Dorothea Dix and Horace Mann worked diligently for this hospital's construction back in the 1830s? Before that, mentally ill people were thrown into jail with criminals and debtors.[58]

If he had been alone, Stephen would have followed the towpath of the Blackstone Canal across town. Now that the weather had cooled, the smell was not as disgusting as in

---

[58] Dorothea Dix (1802-1887) called for humane care of prisoners and the mentally ill in 1840s and worked diligently with her friend Horace Mann (1796-1859) and others to encourage states to build hospitals for the mentally ill. He had earlier established a modern public school system in Massachusetts in 1837 that became a model for the nation.

summer heat. Even though barge traffic had declined with all of the trains coming and going from Worcester, the way Worcester's industries used the waterpower was fascinating. Of course, his stepsister wouldn't understand plodding on a muddy path. At least her skirts did not sweep the sidewalk like his Grandmother's. She actually walked at a decent pace since she was not old enough for corsets and seven layers of petticoats that dragged in the dirt.

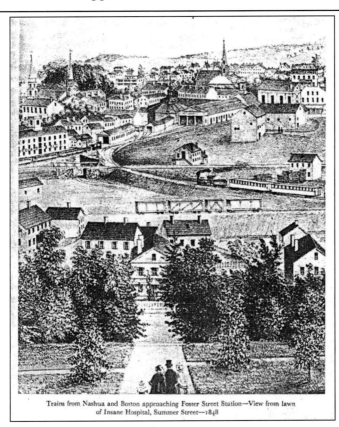

Trains from Nashua and Boston approaching Foster Street Station—View from lawn of Insane Hospital, Summer Street—1848

View from Insane Asylum towards common by steeples on left, station in center and canal behind houses in center.
Tvmeson's *Worcester Centennial. 1848-1948*.

Henry and his father were busy making candy when Stephen and Georgianna arrived at Rawson's fruit and confectionery. Mrs. Rawson answered their call and filled the order. While Stephen pondered over buying a few luscious peaches, Sarah Gleason and Abby, Henry's impish 13-year-old sister, quietly entered the room. Sarah, Henry's beautiful 16-year-old cousin from nearby Princeton, lived with the family so she could go to school and help her aunt and uncle. Her presence was always one of the benefits of Stephen's sweet tooth. [59]

"Stephen, word has it around town that you went into Boston to hear Jenny Lind. Was she as lovely as her voice is reported to be?" Abby greeted him boldly, rudely ignoring his companion.

"Georgianna, I'd like you to meet Mrs. Rawson, Sarah and Abby. Ladies, this is my new stepsister Georgianna", politely putting Abby in her place. Since Stephen always enjoyed watching girls blush, he continued to answer the bold question, "Jenny Lind is as lovely as you, Abby. She has

---

[59] Deering Jones Rawson's middle class family confectionery business was detailed in the 1850 Census showing $500 in real estate and personal estate including 25,000 pounds of sugar worth $2150 and $3,600 value in confections. The 1858 City Directory listed him as a fruit dealer, as well. The Rawsons lived at 7 Grafton Street, but no business location was given. Mrs. Abigail Persis Blanchard Rawson (1811-1895) was involved with the Children's Friend Society for over 37 years. Abby probably attended high school in 1853 before dying the following year. Henry (1834-1886) continued the family candy making business. The family is buried in Hope Cemetery as are the Worcester orphans.

beautiful blue eyes like Sarah here and is just about as tall, I'd guess. Here's the picture I bought to remember the evening."

As both girls eagerly mulled over Jenny Lind's picture (see page 61), Sarah asked, "What song did you like the best?"

Stephen quickly replied, "'The Swedish Herdsman's Song'. I'd never heard it before and her soprano voice held the audience spell bound as she echoed the herdsman's call."

Here the misty mountain
Hearkens to my evening song;
Toward the peaceful valley,
Happy spot! I gaze and long.

Onward flies my view,
Where an azure hue
Tints the distant green
Where in glist'ning sheen
Still the lakelet lies,
And my bosom's prize
Doth shame its blue with bluer eyes.

She little knows
The earnest vows
That echo mocks,
Unto the rocks;
The forest grove
Alone doth prove
A true confession of my love.

For ah!

Alone the barren misty mountain

Hearkens to my evening song;

Toward the peaceful valley,

Happy spot! I gaze and long.

Onward flies my view,

Toward the distant blue,

Fraught with hopeful pray'r

That she dwell 'neath Heaven's care.

Library of Congress.

Band Music from the Civil War Era.

"A Concert for Brass Band, Voice, and Piano".

"Does she really donate most of her income to charities, Stephen?" asked Mrs. Rawson.

"Oh yes, she has even donated to the anti-slavery cause. There are so many things that need to be improved in America. Which reminds me, we're heading over to the Orphans' Home this morning. Are the comfits ready?"

Henry finally appeared from the back room saving him from more of the girls' chatter.

"Mornin', Stephen. Glad I caught you before you left. I just received a letter from Ephraim. He writes the gold fields have yielded little wealth, but plenty of adventure. Do you have a moment to read it?"

"No, we must be on our way," Stephen said and then lowered his voice. "I have Georgianna in tow today. Do you ever think about headin' west, Henry? I sometimes do, but I know my father expects me to attend Harvard University first."

Panning for gold image at Collins Development.
<http://www.collinsdevelopment.com/activities/goldpanning.php>

Henry laughed, "My father expects me to continue makin' candy. Our family doesn't have your resources. Perhaps when I finish my schoolin' and save some money, I'll take advantage of the opportunities out west. People like sweets wherever they live. Sugar is so expensive and more and more abolitionists refuse to eat anything produced by slave labor."

Eaves dropping Abby chimed in, "You boys are lucky to even have a choice. Sarah and I cannot go to college unless we go to Oberlin like Lucy Stone.[60] And Henry, do you think

[60]Lucy Stone (1818-1893) was from West Brookfield, just west of Worcester. She was one of the first Massachusetts' women to graduate from a full course college. Oberlin College in Ohio, first to admit black students in 1835 and female students in 1837, was founded in 1833 under the Congregational Church. After graduating, Stone lectured for an immediate end to slavery and for woman's equality, dedicating her life to making the world a better place.

father would let either of us apprentice his trade? We're destined to be housewives, I'm afraid."

Mrs. Rawson heard the frustrated last comment spoken in a very unladylike voice. "There's hope, Abby. Next week I plan to attend the Woman's Rights Convention at Brinley Hall. We'll be discussing the rightful adjustment of woman's rights, duties, and relationships. I believe Miss Harriot Hunt will speak about medical training for women and Miss Antoinette Brown will speak about women as ministers. I'll need you and Sarah to help prepare supper and care for your brother, but perhaps you could attend the evening sessions with me. Lucy Stone is one of the organizers and will probably speak."

Large smiles blossomed on Abby's and Sarah's lovely faces. Henry and Stephen laughed at this female foolishness as Stephen headed out the door with his sweet treats and his sister.

As they continued on their way, he wondered if the girls really thought men would allow their wives and daughters more freedom. Then again, he thought, his grandmother was a very independent woman. He wondered what Georgianna thought, but didn't bother to ask.

The Orphans' Home was just a few blocks away and Georgianna didn't wait long to ask questions about the Rawsons and this woman's convention. "Do you think MY mother would be interested?"

Caught off guard Stephen realized she was HIS mother now, too. How would it affect their family? He was glad he'd soon be out of the house.

To end the chatter, he bluntly said, "Our mother has a new family and husband to care for. Father would not like her associating with these radicals." He did not add that many of the Unitarian women would probably attend. Why help foster this independent spirit of the age?

Comfits

"Mornin', sir. Mornin', miss," a very plain girl with lots of freckles about Georgianna's age answered the Orphans' Home door.

"Thank you, Liza," Miss White said as she seated Stephen and Georgianna in the parlor. "Perhaps, Mr. Salisbury and the young miss would like a cup of tea?"

They both nodded as they were struck at how different this plain parlor was from the elegant furnishings at their grandmother's. Georgianna looked around and followed Liza with wide eyes. She had never had an experience like this. Her elegant frock was so different from Liza's simple green check dress.   She realized these children really did need the community's help. Nearby, the sound of children's voices drifted in from the schoolroom.

Stephen took immediate control of the conversation, "We've brought some clothing for the boys and girls from my grandmother and father. Grandmother added a special sweet treat, as well. May we give them to the children now, Miss White?"

She pondered for a moment before agreeing. Stephen and Georgianna were led into the schoolroom, but she insisted each child give a brief recitation before receiving a comfit. They dutifully clapped at each child's accomplishment and were rewarded by bright smiles.

As the children finished, Liza announced that tea was served. The guests returned to the parlor to Miss White's praises of their generosity. "Georgianna, Liza is our star pupil. Liza, please choose a reading for our friends from your Second Reader."

"Yes, Miss Gleason. 'The Song of the Bee' by Marian Douglas," began Liza.

> *Buzz! buzz! buzz!*
> *This is the song of the bee.*
> *His legs are of yellow;*
> *A jolly, good fellow,*
>   *And yet a great worker is he.*

In days that are sunny
He's getting his honey;
In days that are cloudy
He's making his wax:
On pinks and on lilies,
And gay daffodillies,
And columbine blossoms,
  He levies a tax!

Buzz! buzz! buzz!
The sweet-smelling clover,
He, humming, hangs over;
The scent of the roses
Makes fragrant his wings:
He never gets lazy;
From thistle and daisy,
And weed of the meadow,
  Some treasure he brings.

Buzz! buzz! buzz!
From morning's first light
Till the coming of night,
He's singing and toiling
  The summer day through.

Oh! We may get weary,
And think work is dreary;
'Tis harder by far
  To have nothing to do.

Everyone had applauded Liza's accomplishments.

On the way home Stephen was moved to remember how closely he and Georgianna shared the loss of a parent as did the orphans. At least he and his step sister were blessed to still have one parent and they must move onward. He could not imagine life without his father and grandmother. He was glad they had spent the day helping others -- some of whom were indeed, helping themselves. Georgianna wasn't really too bad of a companion, after all. Perhaps he'd take her back along the canal path. He could feel the spirit of his mother smiling down from heaven.

How different their world was from mine...

What is love? 'tis not hereafter;
Present mirth hath present laughter;
What's to come is still unsure;
In delay there lies no plenty'
Then come and kiss me, sweet and twenty,
Youth's a stuff will not endure.

Shakespeare's *Twelfth Night* (act 2, scene 3)

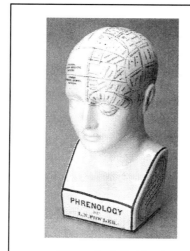

Phrenologist's Head.
Morse's "Facing a Bumpy History".

WIFE OR DOCTOR?

Growing more cramped and numbed in my hiding place at the front of the car, I am warmed by remembrances of Stephen Salisbury's enthusiasm and smile for my accomplishments. This memory brought his schoolmate Emily Loveland to mind. She was always so sure of herself. How often I wished I could visit her home a few blocks away from the Orphans' Home. Could I be like her now? Had the time come to boldly stand instead of burrowing like a scared rabbit?

David and Olive Loveland's Home   October 16, 1850

1 Fulton Street, Worcester

Sixteen-year-old Emily hurried home from the Anti-Slavery Bazaar and came breezing into the kitchen of her family's boarding house.

"Oh, Mother! Why won't Father let us go to the Woman's Rights Convention? There's never been such a convention before! Just think, a chance to discuss only women's issues. Lucretia Mott and Paulina Wright Davis[61] are both coming to town."

"Emily, quit chattering and help put supper on the table. The boarders won't wait forever and your father will never listen to you on an empty stomach. "

"Don't you ever tire of caring for our family and six boarders? I know it helps our family income, but I want to do more with my life. I would like to become a doctor like Elizabeth Blackwell.[62] These are exciting times, mother. Look

---

[61] Paulina Wright Davis (1813-1876), as the only organizer with time, energy and wealth to make the arrangements for the convention, also served as its president of the convention. She lectured on anatomy for women, petitioned for married women's property rights in New York and served in the leadership of the abolitionist movement. She moved to Rhode Island with her second husband in 1853 and published the *Una,* a paper dedicated to women's rights.

[62] Elizabeth Blackwell (1821-1910) was the first woman granted a medical degree in the United States in 1849.

how Worcester has grown and changed since we moved here from New York."

"Serve the hot dishes, NOW, Emily. This is not the time to be dreaming."

Emily wasn't really dreaming. She was practicing what she would say to her father. His mind had been occupied with the lease arrangements of the building on the corner of Front and Summer Streets. Her parents had been eager to close Earl Peck's hole-in-the-wall rum and beer volcano [tavern]. Her father planned to convert the whole premises to some respectable use. Emily truly admired her parents' advocacy of the temperance cause. Her mother was a member of the Ladies' Washingtonian Sewing Circle with Mrs. Rawson.[63]

The Lovelands were very active in the Worcester Anti-Slavery Sewing Circle, as well. Sarah Earle was so pleased her mother would be opening next week's convention that at the last Anti-Slavery Meeting both she and Abby Kelley Foster had added their kind words to encourage Mr. Loveland to let his daughter attend the event. What an honor it would be for Emily to meet Mrs. Mott in person. She had committed her life to the abolition of slavery. Hopefully, Emily's father could be

---

[63] The Lovelands belonged to Worcester County Anti-Slavery Society. An Emilie A. Loveland was recording secretary in 1852 and Olive Landers Loveland (c. 1815-1872) served on the Executive Committee in 1852-1854 of the South Division of the Ladies Anti-Slavery Sewing Circle. Merchant David M. Loveland (1806-1860) was cited as having "temperance principles" in the 7 November 1850 *The Worcester Cataract and Waterfall*, a temperance weekly newspaper.

convinced to let her support the woman's cause as well. These issues were all linked by the idea that every human must be the best possible person one could be and thus make the world a better place. Would all Emily's groundwork pay off?

With confidence and a quick smooth of her skirt, Emily grabbed the bowl brimming with boiled onions and pushed through the door.

Immediately, William Johnson's icy blue eyes melted her heart with a welcoming smile. She could tell he had been waiting for her appearance. Perhaps he would be an ally. Mr. Loveland had been impressed with his good work at Merrifield's[64] as a talented machinist. Emily thought he was so handsome with his light blonde hair and deep blue eyes.

Last summer she had tended to a deep cut on William's finger. Finally, she felt he saw her as an intelligent woman rather than a child. The wound was deep enough to uncover the "worms" of fat padding the blood vessels, tendons and finger bones. As she discussed how the human body was a living machine, William and she found a kindred interest. That night she had written of the incident in her journal and wondered if this was what is meant by the beauty of the mind? She certainly did not consider herself a physical beauty with a

---

[64] Merrifield's was a three-story brick building filling a whole city block owned by William T. Merrifield. It housed more than fifty firms which used steam power for various mechanical manufacturing enterprises.

ruddy complexion and fine dark brown hair that would never stay neatly tucked up, no matter how she tried to arrange it.

Returning for more platters, her cheeks burned with thoughts of William. She mentally warned herself not to become distracted from her quest.

Finally she and her mother joined the others just as Mr. Loveland decided to share a silly poem he found in *The Cataract.* [65]

> *When Eve brought WOE to all mankind,*
> *Old Adam called her wo-man,*
> *But when she WOO'D with love so kind,*
> *He then pronounced her WOO-man.*
> *But now with folly and with pride*
> *Her husbands' pockets trimming,*
> *The ladies are so full of whims,*
> *The people call them WHIM-men.*

The poem wasn't that funny, thought Emily during the hilarious uproar.

"Ouch!" her 10-year old brother Johnny yelled as Emily's swift kick under the table connected with his shin and halted his laughter. The other men, however, were not so easy to stop.

---

[65] "The Gentler Sex," *The Massachusetts Waterfall and Cataract* 14 November 1850 (135).

She took it as a personal insult to her intelligence as a woman. Not to mention that of her mother who never wasted a penny in her life!

With uncharacteristic politeness she withheld the retorts brimming in her mouth and began to eat. Her mind turned inward to her plan to earn her own way as a doctor if she was allowed to study in a medical school.

Or she might give lectures like Mrs. Davis. Her physiology and hygiene lectures were popular even though some in her audiences fainted at the mere sight of her imported French mannequin! How ridiculous! Women, and even girls, needed to understand how their bodies worked.

Over the past year she'd been talking with Mrs. M. S. Thompson and Mrs. Goodwin about midwifery.[66] They each had offered Emily an apprenticeship, but she didn't want to be limited to delivering babies. It still lay within woman's limited sphere of child rearing. Emily felt there was more to be done.

In her second year at Worcester's Classical and English High School Emily had chosen the third course to learn more science and mathematics. As the class studied the United States Constitution, she found herself growing more and more upset that girls were not considered equal citizens because of their sex. Worcester was blessed to have a co-educational

---

[66] Both female physicians were listed in the *1851 City Directory*.

high school.[67]   Most girls at the time did not realize they were legally left out of the democratic process.   Emily thought ignorance held girls back more than anything else.

"*Je continue à explorer la médecine,*" [68] she muttered. Didn't they know she'd been reading books on anatomy and physiology! Just before school began, she had visited the root doctor on nearby Summer Street to hear about that type of medicine.   Mrs. Lucy Schuyler[69] was an expert at finding the correct herbal remedy to help an illness. Emily was able to ask intelligent questions after last year's course in botany.

Her summer's big adventure had been a visit to Dr. Seth Rodgers' hydrotherapy clinic over on Glen Street. This new water-cure had many followers, even the Fosters. Johnny had thought the whole idea was as hilarious as the poem. The very thought of being wrapped in a dripping wet sheet for 45 minutes, followed by a shower and then a pail of 75 degree water dumped over one's shoulders was a shivering thought. No wonder the patient was ready to exercise vigorously! She firmly agreed that drinking copious amounts of clear water was

---

[67] After passing the entrance exam Emily attended Worcester Classical and English High School at the corner of Walnut and Oak Streets.

[68] "I also continue my self-exploration of medicine."

[69] Reverend Peter Schuyler was a preacher at the African Methodist Episcopal Church and active in the Underground Railroad. He and Lucy lived at 158 Summer Street and both shared a medical office on Court Street according to the *1851 City Directory*.

better for one's health than some of the common alcoholic cordials. All of these new ideas in medicine were as exciting to Emily as the new inventions in the factories were to William and Johnny.

Supper passed quickly as she day-dreamed and tried to avoid William's eyes. Sometimes she thought her father read poems like that just to tease her. This time she had conquered her temper, like a perfect lady. Well, except for kicking Johnny. After supper she would take control of the moment to enlighten the "gentlemen."

After the women finished the dishes, they joined the others sitting on the porch to savor the crisp fall evening.[70] It was the best time of year with few insects buzzing in eyes and ears.

William gallantly stood and greeted, "If your mother had let me help with the dishes, we could have had more time together, Emily."

The others hooted.

"William, the world is not ready for man to be a kitchen drudge," commented Ben Hooper, one of the other boarders.

"Perhaps next Wednesday's convention will adjust your thinking," Emily boldly countered, seizing the moment of attack. "Work is always completed faster when shared and the drudgery is less burdensome. Lucy Stone believes husbands

---

[70] The sun set at 5:30 p.m. that week and there was a full moon on 20th at about 10:30 p.m. according to Howland's *1850 Worcester Almanac*.

and wives should be helpmates as in colonial times or as the pioneering couples do out west. Both partners help farm, build a shelter, contribute income and meet the survival needs of the family."

"Be realistic, Emily," her father put her in her place. "Worcester and towns all over New England now have an industrial economy. The agrarian economy of Thomas Jefferson's view is dying. Husbands must go out to earn a living. It is up to the wife to tend the children and manage the household."

"What about the poorer families, Mr. Loveland?" William said coming to her rescue. "Even the children must go off to work for the family to survive. It makes more sense to me to have a family where husband and wife are coequals. Mrs. Loveland's wonderful meals and comfortable rooms are certainly an asset to your financial endeavors and reform efforts. You both are active Washingtonians and strive to end the alcoholic abuses that contribute to keeping the poor downtrodden."

"I see your point, William. Is this what you think will be discussed at the convention, Emily?"

"Yes, Father. It disgusts me that a drunken, abusive father has legal guardianship over his children, just because of his sex. If woman's morality is so honored by our society, why doesn't the legal system support her wisdom to make the best choices for her children as the father's co-equal? After all, it took two people to make the babe."

"Enough, Emily!" scolded her mother as she tactfully changed the subject to a more ladylike topic. "I really appreciate your taking my place at the Anti-Slavery Fair over at Brinley Hall since I felt poorly this afternoon, dear. How were the sales?"

"We are doing very well, Mother. I saw Mrs. Rawson and she invited me to go to the Woman's Rights Convention with her and Miss Gleason from the Orphans' Home, if you give your consent. She had just heard Dr. Hunt from Boston will be attending and knows I am interested in medicine. Mrs. Clough is also going. Why don't you come, too, Mother?"

"Mr. Loveland, with your permission, I'd take great pleasure in escorting the ladies to the evening sessions," chimed in William.

"I'm sure you would, William," Mr. Loveland chuckled. "Mother and I will discuss this adventure. The women will appreciate your point of view. In the meantime, with all those females, you may even find a wife."

As if on cue, William asked permission to take Emily for a walk with Johnny along as chaperone. Her father waved them off the porch to be rid of all this equal rights talk, Emily thought.

Front Street Bridge over Blackstone Canal at an earlier busier time.
Knowlton's Worcester's Best (250).

Johnny immediately took charge of the conversation asking, "Emily, when you're a doctor, will you 'read' my head? Sam's father had Dr. Fowler, the phrenologist, read the bumps on his head!"

"I won't be that kind of doctor! How can a person's character traits be determined by physical factors? It's as foolish as the men who make generalities about a woman's intellectual and physical abilities based on her size. About the only good thing to say about phrenology is it might encourage people to improve their weaknesses."

William squeezed Emily's arm in support as they paused on the bridge over the canal waters. Johnny was already gathering stones to throw at debris floating in the unused waterway.   Soon this portion of the canal would be covered so the neighborhood would no longer have to put up with the summer stench or danger of children drowning.

Thankfully, Johnny became bored and ran ahead into the darkness. The couple noticed the full moon rising and forgot all discussion. Emily thought, "What a foolish head I have with or without bumps! My heart over-rode my brain once more."

"The evening is finally as calm and beautiful as you, Emily," William leaned close to whisper. "I wish your eyes glowed for me like they do when you speak of the convention. You positively flare with passion when you discuss equality for yourself and for the slaves. I suppose I cannot feel exactly the same since no one has ever denied my rights. I hope your father will let me escort you next week. I fear our time together will end if you go away to a medical school."

She shivered from his words. The chilly breeze blew dry leaves against them and she pulled her shawl closer as they stepped upon the front porch. Everyone had gone inside, but the couple had no desire to join them. Emily worried she would be unable to control her blushing with William so near and excused herself to go to her room to study.

"Study! Ha!" she gasped as she closed her bedroom door. Her spirits were buoyed up and all aglow with present bliss and lively expectations for the future. The cold room and the harsh thought of sacrificing a man who loved her did not beckon. Would she end up a spinster for not responding to William's dreams? Was not the role of woman to be the dutiful wife? Yet, he urged her to follow her dreams. Was he just wooing her heart?

Her father obviously still considered her too young to even imagine such an alliance.[71] How long would William wait? This thought kept Emily wide awake most of the night while she awaited her father's decision about the convention.

---

[71] According to *Massachusetts, Town and Vital Records, 1620-1988* and *Genealogy of the Loveland family in the United States of America ...*, Volume 2 at Ancestry.com, Emily Antoinette Loveland (1834-1869) married lawyer George Mellen Prentiss is 1858. Her interest in medicine is the creation of the author.

"You live in the *nineteenth* century, and are to aid in forming character for the *twentieth*."

William A. Alcott, *Letters to a Sister on Woman's Mission,* 1850.

"For woman's best is unbegun!
Her advent yet to come!"

Abby Hills Price's closing words in her address to the first National Woman's Rights Convention, 23 October 1850 reported by Ebenezer Elliot in *The North Star*, 3 October 1850.

Elizabeth Cady Stanton addresses first woman's rights convention
in 1848 with the Motts seated behind her.
Courtesy of a Women's Rights National Historical Park
Service, New York flyer.

NEVER DID MEN SO SUFFER[72]

Brinley Hall   Evening of October 24, 1850

Main Street, Worcester

     Emily's father laughingly had given Emily permission to
attend the national gathering of men and women to discuss the
issue of women's rights. He was himself committed to making
the world a better place be ending the use of alcohol in his
community and ending slavery in his country. He loved teasing
Emily because she always responded strongly when
challenged—blushing or stating her opinion. His wife

---

[72] From Paulina Wright Davis' *A History of the National Woman's Rights Movement, for Twenty years, with the Proceeding of the Decade Meeting Held at Apollo Hall, October 20, 1870, From 1850 to 1870.*

constantly reminded him it was a father's duty to encourage his daughter, as well as his son, to practice speaking within a loving family before they could comfortably speak for reform in public. He knew William would be a proper escort for Emily and his wife.

"There must be at least a thousand people here tonight, William!" Emily exclaimed while using her fan aggressively to stir the air warmed outside by Indian summer temperatures and inside by the crush of bodies. "The crowd has been growing at each session as news spreads about our discussions. It's a shame so many cannot escape from their necessary labors until the evening sessions. At least father allowed me to miss classes so I could meet people like the famous Mr. Garrison. Father could hardly believe I was in line just behind Mr. Garrison as we signed the register as voting members of the convention."

"I'm pleased your father allowed you to attend the meeting with me, Emily. I must tell you, however, I'm not too disappointed your mother could not join us this evening," said William with a light touch on her sleeve. "Looks like everyone else had the same idea to arrive early to find seats. I wonder why the organizers didn't find a larger hall? At least it will help limit the number of curious rabble rousers," William said, scanning the room.[73]

---

[73] Both Emily and William signed in as members of the convention, although there may have been another William Johnson in Worcester at the time. She

Emily was unconcerned about the problem and let her eyes wander over the sea of strange and familiar faces after they settled into seats next to Mrs. Rawson and Miss Gleason. Mrs. Loveland had looked forward to hearing what her friends would share about the convention at next Friday's sewing circle. The reports in the newspapers had not all been accurate—and some downright insulting.

"Oh look, William, there are Mrs. Clough and Mrs. Powers. I'm glad they are here since we have been discussing the resolution that 'women are clearly entitled to the right of suffrage without distinction of sex or color.' Look how people stare at them, even in this reform-minded crowd. You'd think they were fugitives or slaves. Some of these newcomers did not hear the powerful words of Mr. Douglass and Sojourner Truth this afternoon. Sojourner Truth sure put everyone to laughing when she said, 'It's not fair to let woman suffer because she ate the apple, and to say that she was the weaker vessel, and turned the world upside down accordingly. If she had really done so, what should hinder her to turn it back gain?

---

was #131 and he was #179 on the register of voting members so they probably didn't stand in line together. The organizers had tried to move the convention to the new City Hall (see page 79), but gas lighting was being installed at the time.

Nothing but the intolerance of man.' I think many people bought her narrative[74] after she spoke."

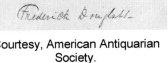

Courtesy, American Antiquarian Society.

Courtesy, American Antiquarian Society.

"You're right, there's certainly nothing stagnant about the atmosphere here with all these women's rights men, like Douglass and Garrison, stirring the waters along with these strong-minded women, Emily."

Emily turned to Miss Gleason, "I'm so pleased Mrs. Earle was asked to open the convention yesterday morning. It shows the country how earnestly our anti-slavery group works towards ending this great evil. Did Sarah Earle tell you she plans to attend Framingham Normal School? If she has a

---

[74] Sojourner Truth (c. 1797- 1883) sold her newly published *Narrative of Sojourner Truth, a Northern Slave* for twenty-five cents to pay off the mortgage on her house in Florence (Northampton), Massachusetts.

college diploma, she thinks the School Committee will have to pay her a better wage. These speeches certainly make me feel like anything is possible if one sets her mind to it."

William laughed, "Especially women like Dr. Hunt?"[75]

Harriot K. Hunt.
Massachusetts Historical
Society.<www.masshist.org>.

"I dare you to find anyone who could argue with her no nonsense reasoning that there are a 'thousand situations in which a mother needs medical knowledge, or the assistance of one of her own sex on whose superior knowledge she can rely.' I totally agree 'that the medical colleges may be opened to

---

[75] Dr. Harriot Kezia Hunt (1805-1875) was a self-taught practicing doctor in Boston who was trying to attend Harvard Medical College to further her education. Following the Convention, she was accepted, but the protests of the male students hindered her attendance.

Mind, not to sex.' Look how high my high school entrance exam scores were. If given a chance to show one's intellect, girls should be allowed to gain a higher education. Were you threatened by the thought of even a female president as Mrs. Foster suggested, William?"

"Well, I think we can also agree girls can marry and be strong-minded, too, after the bantering of the Fosters last night," William pointed out. "I share Mr. Foster's position that husband and wife should be coequals, but it's quite a stretch to put a woman in the White House."

Mrs. Rawson caught his comment and smiled at Emily to whisper, "Dear, if you find a man willing to drop the word 'obey' from your marriage vows, grab him. Life is more pleasant and meaningful with a true partner."

Just then Miss Gleason pointed to a disturbance in the back of the hall caused by the arrival of Lucy Stone. "I hope Miss Stone will say a few words on this final night of the convention she helped organize. I hear she's recovering from a bout of typhoid fever. It's truly a miracle she has energy to even attend."

"Nothing short of death could have stopped her," confided Mrs. Rawson. "It's been half a year since she, Mrs. Foster, Mrs. Davis and concerned others decided to call for this national convention. Following the Annual New England Anti-Slavery Society Convention, they felt something needed to be done about woman's lack of liberty, too. Don't you think it was shrewd of Mrs. Davis to state up front this convention would be more than a declaration of rights and wrongs? That's what Mrs. Stanton and Mrs. Mott did in the *Declaration of Sentiments* at the first convention at Seneca Falls, New York two years ago. What an uproar it made in the papers at the time."

"Indeed, I do. Mrs. Foster certainly did more when she riled up everyone yesterday. Imagine comparing women reformers to the revolutionary patriots who rose up to cut the tyrants' throat," William chimed in, drawing his hand across his throat. "I could vividly imagine you ladies holding a knife to my throat if I did not treat you as my equal. I can understand her defensive stance, though. She's faced stones and rotten eggs thrown by ruffians, as well as the hurtful silent treatment from 'proper ladies' as she's traveled across the country. But as a Quaker, I doubt she was calling for actual bloodshed against the tyranny of our legislators who deny her equal citizenship."

Emily giggled saying, "The letter read from Mrs. Stanton wasn't much better when she called the Senators 'male dolts.' The women of New York are very frustrated in their petition campaign for married property rights. How the state legislators delay! One would think fathers would wish to protect their daughter's inheritance from shiftless husbands. It's all about power and control! Why can't men and women work together as partners? "

"That's where Abby Price's[76] speech hit home. There isn't a man alive who can live without 'the mother who bore him, the playmate of his childhood or the daughter of his love.' I was impressed by her powerful, well-chosen words. I wish I could speak as well," said Miss Gleason. "The children at the Home would not need our help, if everyone acted less selfishly."

"But doesn't it all come down to the right to have a say in our representative democracy?" Emily boldly asked. "The ballot is the key to gaining power. Petitions are easily ignored as we have come to see. Even Mrs. Mott has finally added her support to demanding suffrage. The women of New York could not stop the new property rights law from being repealed because the legislators felt no pressure to carry it into action."

William lent his support. "That's exactly the trouble with asking for something, Emily. The petitioner is always at the mercy of the person with the power. He or she has little to negotiate with. Mothers must plant the seeds of equality in the cradle and hope they will ripen as their sons mature. Otherwise, we ourselves need to bring light to the darkness of the age."

---

[76] Abby Hills Price (1814-1878) was a poet and hymn writer who helped found the utopian Christian community of Hopedale, Massachusetts.

Ernestine Rose in Kolmerten's
The American Life of Ernestine L. Rose.

"Well said, William," Sarah Earle said as she joined our conversation. "These women brave enough to speak before promiscuous audiences have certainly learned the art of effective argument the hard way. They use examples everyone can identify with. We certainly observed why Ernestine Rose[77] is known as 'the queen of the platform' in New York. Who can argue with her point that when woman suffers or man suffers, they BOTH suffer from the inequality? She reminded everyone

---

[77] Ernestine Rose (1810-1892) emigrated from Poland by way of Great Britain where she became a disciple of Robert Owen. As a rabbi's daughter, she was highly educated and at sixteen had defended herself in court to control her inheritance from her mother rather than giving it up as the dowry in an arranged marriage.

that we're fighting for the rights of all humanity, not just one group."

"Ladies, I think you're missing the point. Did you see the Boston *Daily Mail* this morning?" queried William. "No, one is listening outside of the reform circle. Why the *Mail* and other unfriendly press are laughing at us, calling this convention a 'Grand Demonstration of Petticoatdom', and a "motley gathering of fanatical mongrels, of old grannies, male and female, of fugitive slaves and fugitive lunatics".[78]

"Oh, William, that's terrible!" gasped Miss Gleason. "It is so important for America to hear the true message--even if it disturbs the listeners."

"But the press wants to sell papers, so poking fun at these serious speeches and resolutions is part of the game as they see it. Of course, Mrs. Foster's colorful images sell papers, as well." Sarah pointed out as she hurriedly excused herself for the leaders seemed ready to begin.

Emily silently thought, that's why I always try to read and listen with a critical eye and ear. Every word uttered carries a message to favor the speaker. Why even here, the leaders of the convention do not always agree with the words and tactics used to gain the reform they all agree is needed.

---

[78]New York *Herald* 28 October 1850.

RAP!

RAP...RAP...RAP!!

The banging gavel gradually brought a hush to the opening of the final session. Vice President William Henry Channing[79] gave a thrilling and powerful address on how woman is the remedy against the sin of incorrect behavior by man. He then read the resolutions that had been discussed over the past two days.

William Henry Channing.
Wikipedia. <en.wikipedia.org>.

"AYE!" resounded throughout the hall and out the open windows as they were all unanimously adopted. The final one reminded everyone "the million and a half slave women at the South...needed a share in the rights we were claiming for

---

[79] William Henry Channing (1810-1884), not to be confused with his Uncle William Ellery Channing, resigned as Unitarian minister to lead and take part in various reformist societies, including Brooke Farm, Massachusetts.

ourselves." It was a glorious moment for all the people active in the anti-slavery movement.

The next business swiftly confirmed the appointments to the Central Committee, which would call the next convention, and the Committees on Education, Industrial Avocations, Civil and Political Functions, Social Relations and Publication. Each of these working committees were to move the resolutions into action against the traditions that restrain equality for women and Blacks. Emily was proud to be part of this historic moment.

From the stage a Mrs. Tyndale said, "My children ask me how I can expose myself to this audience. I tell them it is to encourage my sisters to accomplish all they can in life, just as I have encouraged my own children. It is my duty to share how I employ my skills in running one of the largest China establishments in this country. I did not choose this path voluntarily, but of necessity. When my husband passed away in Philadelphia, he was deeply in debt. My options were limited, but I was not swayed from the world of business by naysayers, although often tempted. For my perseverance, I have been blessed with success."

While many in the audience wept at her moving story, practical Miss Gleason whispered to Mrs. Rawson, "Now, this is just the type of encouragement women need to hear to realize they need not take low paying jobs or choose the life of the street. But one needs education to take on the work. Perhaps we could train our more astute students for business."

As Emily mentally added "and for medicine" to Miss Gleason's remarks, a small woman dressed in black stood to echo her thoughts. She told the audience she was a female physician of Providence, Rhode Island. Emily had not realized how many women had braved this difficult path--and succeeded. She caught William staring at her as he listened and he smiled as if reading her mind.

A ripple of excitement ran through the audience as Lucy Stone[80] finally took the platform. She had been known to hold an audience spell-bound for three to five hours when healthy.

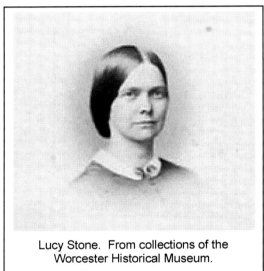

Lucy Stone. From collections of the Worcester Historical Museum.

---

[80] Lucy Stone (1818-1893) was one of the first women from Massachusetts to earn a college degree. She spoke out for women's rights and against slavery. She helped organize the 1850 convention, but became ill with typhoid and many feared she would be unable to attend. Stone was the first recorded American woman to retain her own last name after marriage.

I had great misgivings about the success such a national gathering could have in changing the balance of humanity in our nation," she began in a bell-like voice. "Hearing the resolutions passed this evening, however, shows it has been a triumphant success. Woman must take her rights as far as she can get them; but those she cannot take she must ask for –demand in the name of a common humanity. We must circulate petitions for the Right of Suffrage and Right of married Women to hold Property.

We <u>want</u> to be something more than the appendages of Society; we <u>want</u> that Woman should be the coequal and help-meet of Man in all the interests, and perils and enjoyments of human life. We <u>want</u> that she should attain to the development of her nature and womanhood, we <u>want</u> that when she dies, it may not be written on her grave-stone that she was the 'relict' of somebody.[81]

Deafening applause shook the building. Emily's heart was bursting with the possibilities of achieving the "wants" in her lifetime. What a world it could be!

Several speakers followed, but could not match the power of Miss Stone. As the hour to adjourn approached Lucretia Mott rose to make the closing address.

---

[81] Rather than known by her own name.

Courtesy, American Antiquarian Society.

Let us dwell a moment on the simple and truthful words of Sojourner Truth, the poor woman who had grown up under the curse of Slavery, 'Goodness is from everlasting and will never die, while evil has a beginning and must come to an end.'"

Are ye able to bear all the mountains of difficulty that stand in the way of this reform? Mark the words of Jesus, 'Lift up your eyes and behold the harvest, white for the reaper. Pray ye that laborers may be sent into the harvest.' (John 4:35 in Bible)

We must be living agents of this work. The age has come. Look at the success of the Temperance and Anti-Slavery reforms.

We have met around this altar of humanity, and though no vocal prayers have been offered, one has arisen from our hearts. And now Lord, let thy servants depart in peace; 'for our eyes have seen thy salvation.' (Luke 2:30 in *Bible*)

Buoyed by the evening's excitement, Emily and William said their good-byes with great exuberance. Strolling the few blocks home, William let Emily babble about her plans to continue her pursuit of medical training. Finally, they turned the corner on Washington Square where Mrs. Rawson and Miss Gleason split off from the group towards their homes.

"I'm not a patient man, Emily. But we are young and I cannot yet earn enough to support you and your dreams. I'll never make you promise to obey me except in this: always be my friend. My love for you will never diminish," William said quietly as he stooped to kiss Emily.

Emily went to bed content.[82]

---

[82] A William H. Johnson boarded with the Lovelands according to the 1850 Census Another William was listed with middle initial W. in the 1850 City Directory and moved to the Franklin House per the 1851 Worcester Street Directory. The story of their friendship is the creation of the author based on stories of other woman's rights men.

There is not a lunatic asylum in the country, wherein, if the inmates were called together to sit in convention, they would not exhibit more sense, reason, decency and delicacy, and less of lunacy, blasphemy, and horrible sentiments, than this hybrid, mongrel, pie-bald, crack- brained, pitiful, disgusting and ridiculous assemblage....may God have mercy on their miserable souls. Amen.

New York Herald, 28 October 1850

HARVESTING NEW IDEAS

Continuing to gather strength to deal with my impending doom, I think back on the day a barrel of apples were delivered by Dr. Woodward. Miss White rallied the whole house into action except for the little ones sent outside with Persis and Jimmy. It was not the hard work, but the conversation stimulated by Miss Gleason's account of the first National Woman's Rights Convention, that opened new gates for my mind to wander through.

Orphans' Home   October 25, 1850

Pine Street, Worcester

"The crowd kept filling the hall around us. People were standing against the walls and in every corner. I know you didn't want me to take off, but it was good we arrived early so we had seats," Miss Gleason commented to Miss White while stirring a huge kettle of applesauce so it wouldn't burn. "Many of our friends were present to hear what the speakers had to say about woman's rights."

Miss White sourly replied as she sorted out the unbruised apples to keep in the root cellar, "My dear, I feel the whole exercise was just wasted breath. I'm amazed Mrs. Earle was associated with it. I thought anti-slavery was her cause."

We girls were all busy with the apples, but my ears had perked up at the mention of my idol's family as I continued coring apples and passing them to Mary to slice. She would then relay them to the younger girls to thread onto a cord so we could hang them up to dry until we needed them during the winter.

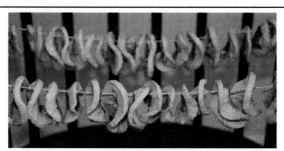

Experiments in Efficiency.
<http://efficiencyexperiments.blogspot.com>(2013).

"Almost the whole Earle family was present in the front row", continued Miss Gleason. "Did you read the articles in *The Spy*? Mrs. Earle gave a very warm welcome to people who came from around the United States to Worcester, even the newer states of California and Iowa."

"I remember Sarah Earle told us her mother's cousin, Lucretia Mott, would be staying at their home," added Miss White. "It's hard to believe ten years have passed since Mrs. Mott and the other female American delegates were denied the right to sit with the other delegates at the World's Anti-Slavery Convention in England. It was this prejudice against women acting outside of their homes and local woman's groups that led to the first woman's rights meeting in Seneca Falls, New York, two years ago when Mrs. Mott was visiting her sister and Mrs. Stanton."

"No one can ever bring about the end of a great wrong like slavery, if they are restricted in their actions to signing petitions," huffed Miss Gleason. "Why, even the Children's Friend Society had to appeal to the legislature to gain the right to act as guardians and Mother Miles had to go door to door pleading for support."

"Yes, it was a means to an end," sighed Miss White. "This very home the result of our actions. However, those convention resolutions promise to be a long rocky path to travel. It's like chasing the wind and we have other more important daily concerns."

"Oh come now, Miss White. "Our work is very important, but no change will ever happen if the waters are not stirred by open discussion. Think of how difficult it is to change the lives of all the poor children who cannot live with us. The mothers want to care for their children, but have no power against the law which entitles their husband total authority. It's like they are almost a 'slave driver.' We must educate the public about the problem. Most women accept their lot for there is no way to overcome tradition. The convention resolved to form a Central Committee to call future annual meetings, gather information and publish it for the public. It's the beginning of a movement across the country!"

"Hah, but who will read the resolutions?" Miss White challenged. "Look at how they poke fun at the speeches in the papers. Calling the leaders crowing hens. And what did you think of Mrs. Price's speech? Is she grounded in reality living in that utopian Hopedale community?"

"She cut to the core of the matter," countered Miss Gleason. Mrs. Price feels there are four areas of concern and the meeting resolved that these would be the next steps for action: equal education, equal vocational opportunities, equality before the law and better social relationships."

Silently, I pondered these four concerns as they related to my own life. I had already discovered I did not have access to the same education as Sarah Earle, Abby Rawson and Emily Loveland. So I was two steps behind most girls, as was Becca.

In addition, what vocational opportunities did I have? Cooking, cleaning, caring for children and laundry were my lot even at eight years old. And wasn't that the role of every wife? They didn't even receive any pay for their efforts. My sister Mary, Mrs. Powers, Mrs. Clough and Miss Jane, our cook, were the only women I knew who received pay for this work. And then, they all had their own household tasks to do in addition. Well, except Mary who felt like she had no life of her own as Mrs. Mile's servant. What must I know to open my own shop like Charlie Clough and his father?

Miss Gleason was telling about Frederick Douglass and Sojourner Truth when I stopped daydreaming. I remembered he was the slave boy who had taught himself to read. Mr. Douglass had also attended the Seneca Falls Convention, but Worcester was the first time Sojourner Truth had spoken on woman's rights. Seems she had the crowd laughing when she said it wasn't fair to let woman suffer because she ate the apple in the Garden of Eden and turned the world upside down.

We all knew that *Bible* story, but Miss Gleason giggled as she continued Sojourner Truth's speech, 'If Eve had really done so, what should hinder her to turn it back again? Nothing but the intolerance of man!'"

"Whoa, the preachers aren't going to like those words at all," cautioned Miss White as several of us joined the laughter.

"These men and women weren't afraid to state the truth, Miss White! I do fear, however, the strong language will scare away many who are sympathetic to the need for reform and equality."

"Equality before the law!" exclaimed Miss Jane. "Now there's a hopeless quest. What male legislator would give up any power to a woman? I heard they even included the phrase 'without distinction of sex or race. Won't this anger the women in the south? Imagine what the slave owners are saying!"

"I know, but Mrs. Stanton had sent a letter to the convention saying America could 'gladly forego one-half the male dolts now serving' in Congress if women could vote and were free of domestic work. The discussion always seemed to return to the necessity of equal education. Then all humans can share their talents for the good of all. Every human has something to contribute and should not be limited by tradition."

"But married women won't use the right to vote as we single women would. Their husbands will just tell them how to cast their ballot."

Miss White always seemed to dampen Miss Gleason's excitement, but Miss Gleason did not give up. "I disagree. Look at the mothers who have been forced to leave their children here. Their husbands are dead or run off. They are struggling to survive and should be able to choose their lawmakers. We need more women like Mrs. Stanton and Mrs. Rose working with legislators to change arbitrary laws that deny women control of their own income and inheritance. Laws that give husbands the right to beat their wives like slaves. Laws that give fathers total guardianship of their children for their own gain. There is no legal partnership in a marriage."

"What madness did Mrs. Foster spout? Mrs. Rawson seemed mightily upset."

"Abby Kelley Foster hasn't changed one bit, Miss White. She said women have the right to rise up against the tyrants just as our forefathers did against King George. Her analogy would have worked well, but once on the roll she used the phrase 'cut the tyrants' throats.' The idea of bloodshed in this reform effort was totally unacceptable, but it certainly captured everyone's imagination. I think it was the only time Brinley Hall was totally silent."

Miss White gasped and literally turned white, "What nerve that woman has!"

I, however, was still thinking about Charlie Clough's granddaddy and Isaiah Thomas fighting against King George and Da's hatred of the British king. "Miss Gleason, did women raise knives in the war for independence?" I blurted out.

Miss White glared at my impertinence.

Miss Gleason, always ready to give a history lesson, told us about Molly Pitcher taking over for her husband on the battlefield and pioneer women protecting their children by firing flintlocks and bearing pitchforks against Indian attacks. "Women can be as strong as is necessary, ladies. Your actions must rise to meet every occasion! But," she cautioned, "think about the effect your words will have before they leave your lips. I think Mrs. Foster's choice of words startled the entire audience into a more serious level of thought. However, many feared the extreme radicals might rule the day. Thankfully, calmer heads were in control like Mrs. Mott."

"Who else was there?" Cindy quietly asked as she rolled out pie dough under Miss Jane's supervision.

"Well, I shouldn't spread gossip, but you all know Emily Loveland. She was there with that handsome boarder at her parent's house. She was positively beaming when I saw her being introduced to Dr. Harriot Hunt. Dr. Hunt gave a rousing speech about 'educating the Mind, not the sex.' What difference does the body housing the brain make? She had been very upset about being denied the opportunity to attend lectures at Harvard Medical School even though she is a respected physician in Boston. I fear that young man has nary a chance against Emily's medical curiosity."

"Becca said her aunts all attended the convention," Mary mentioned.

"Oh yes, Mrs. Clough, Mrs. Powers and several women from their church were present. Mrs. Clough has high expectations for her children. We all agree that's the key. If you don't strive for the best, you will not rise above the darkness of stagnation," said Miss Gleason enthusiastically.

"Speaking of education Louisa, did Lucy Stone make the convention?" asked Miss White. "I heard she was seriously ill? She's a wonderful speaker and one of the few female college graduates here in Massachusetts."

One time Abby Rawson had told me how Miss Stone gathered wild berries and nuts to save for her education. She then had to teach school to earn enough for her tuition at Oberlin College because her father did not think girls needed all that learning. That had been my plan before Mary had suggested the Lowell mills as a quicker source of income.

"Yes, she spoke powerfully about the success of the convention. She reminded everyone that 'what we want is not to be mere appendages of society, but co-equals and helpmates in all aspects of life.' Now, wouldn't you all agree that's not too radical of a goal?"[83]

As I busted out another apple core, I pondered my importance like an arm or a leg doing all the jobs necessary to run a household. I was treated differently because I am Irish and a girl, not to mention a child. It seemed the only way to not be someone else's arms and legs, like a beast of burden, was to learn how to think and speak. If you can use the power of words to sway people's opinions and find answers to difficult questions, you are needed regardless of your sex, where you came from or even the color of your skin.

---

[83] The ladies' comments in this chapter are a composite of similar responses from the time found in letters, diaries, journals and newspaper articles of the time.

My thoughts are interrupted by shouting in the back of the car. Do I want to be found weak and shaking or is it time for me "to lift up my voice like a trumpet", as the *Bible* says? (Isaiah 58:1 in *Bible*)

MOVING ONWARD

Foster Street Station   January 20, 1853

Worcester, Massachusetts

"Ouch!" A vise-like grip on my arm jerks me out of my reveries before I can act on my thoughts.

"Come on, Miss," a giant constable with a big nose commands while pulling me up from the floor. "Yer certainly causing a fuss."

Shivering even though I felt no cold, I try to gain my balance and look towards the opposite end of the car where Mary and I had boarded. Where is she? My muscles tingle and ache from being crouched in my hiding place under the front seat. I can neither move nor stop the tears creeping down my face. All the strong women I had been remembering could not prevent the flood. The car had filled and a sea of strange faces stare at me. Their curiosity and disgust are plainly evident.

"I'm so sorry." I whisper over and over as we walk the length of the car. I unsteadily ease down the steps to face my angry faced benefactress, Mother Miles, and my sister Mary standing on the platform below.

Mary holds her head high as she insists, "I was only doing what I thought was best for Liza and me. I knew you would not like the plan, so I did not bother to discuss it with you for fear you'd stop us. And here you are."

Mother Miles' face is contorted by anger and hurt. Mary has been almost a member of their family for four years. Mother Miles had put her reputation and that of the Children's Friend Society on the line by arranging my indenture with the Burbank family. Taking a deep breath, she sternly dismisses Mary. "We'll discuss it at home. Come along."

The constable bends over to pick up our carpetbag. Does he think we will continue to run?

CLANG! CLANG! CLANG!

"Last call. All-l-l-l-l-l aboard!"

We all jump at the warning bell of the Nashua train. It will pull out without us!

Whoo-oo-oo … SH-h-h-h-h…

Suddenly, Mary snatches the valise and hops onto the bottom step of the moving train. "I'm sorry, Liza. I just can't go back," she yells over the noisy mechanical sounds of departure. "I'll write…."

The puckered expression on Mother Miles' face and glare of the constable would have been funny at any other moment. I cannot believe Mary has left me to face the consequences alone.

Mother Miles marches me out of the station, triumphant in the capture of her fugitive indentured servant. Mary's action shocks my tears away. I must be brave and stand up for my wishes. However, I cannot look Jimmy in the eye as we pass him to board the waiting hack.

Here I am back where my life began in Worcester three years ago!

"I'll let you know if we decide to press charges, Constable Walter. Thank you for your assistance."

With a nod and a grim smile my way, he leaves us standing in the Miles' parlor.

"I need a cup of tea, Liza, before I can tackle this serious matter. Come along to the kitchen. What a dilemma you have caused," she huffs as we storm down the hall.

"What are YOU doing here? Louisa Miles demands. "What's wrong Mother?"

I can tell she's in a foul mood since it's Mary's day off and she must prepare dinner. I ignore her and plead, "Mother Miles, I apologize again for trying to take the easy way out of my problems by running away. Mary was only trying to make our dreams come true."

"Louisa, be a dear and pour Liza and me a cup of tea. This is a private matter."

I know enough to hide my smile. It will not pay to have more enemies.

"Dreams?" Mother Miles responds. "I cannot believe you felt you could not discuss your troubles with me, Miss Gleason or Miss White before making such a rash decision. Your sister acted very irresponsibility for a 22-year-old woman. However, I suppose we cannot fault you too much for following her lead. I thought Mary was content working for our family."

"Mr. Courtney hurt her feelings," I whisper. "He didn't love her enough to go against his family. Please don't be angry."

Since Ma always told us that honesty is the best policy because the Lord always sees the Truth, I took a deep breath and accepted my fate, "I'm the criminal. I almost broke my indenture contract. So I'll meet Mr. Burbank this afternoon as planned."

"You certainly will, young lady! What an embarrassment. I suppose we can keep this incident between ourselves. However, my household will be in turmoil without Mary."

The reminder that Mary is gone suddenly gives me backbone to speak up firmly. "Forgive me, Mother Miles. I'm heartily sorry for insulting the kindness and care I received at the Orphans' Home for the past three years. I was not running from that. In fact, I miss the chance to learn more than anything. Miss White and Miss Gleason opened my eyes to the importance of knowledge. Mary said I could earn enough money in the mill to continue my education. The Burbanks aren't going to let me to attend the local school anymore. Seven years is too long to wait for my contract to end! Mrs. Burbank doesn't even allow me a decent candle to read. 'Need my sleep more than book learnin,' sez she."

Mother Miles face softens slightly. "Why didn't you tell anyone how you felt, Eliza?"

"No one ever asked my opinion. The Board of Managers always seems eager to place us in a home as soon as we turn eleven so the Home won't be too crowded. And everyone seemed so pleased I would be working and living near my brother and sister. Me, too--at first. Adults have always been in control of my life, so I never thought to speak up. I feared Reform School like poor Joey if I caused trouble."

Emboldened by her momentary sympathy, I struggle on to make myself understood. "I understand I am a criminal for breach of contract. Is there no way out of it? Could I remain in the Home to continue my studies? I could help teach the children now that I am older. Could I take Mary's place here and attend school with Abby Rawson and Emily Loveland? I would work doubly hard even though I am only eleven. I promise I'll never embarrass you again, Mother Miles."

"Well, dear, you are in no position to bargain. Your sister is obviously old enough to find her own way in life. You, on the other hand, continue to be my responsibility and burden. You will spend tonight at the Home. Do not discuss this matter with any of the children. I'll meet Mr. Burbank this afternoon at the time he expects to pick you up here. We must not make a hasty decision like Mary has done. My day has already been turned topsy-turvy, but I am not cruel and heartless. Think of all the trouble that could have been avoided if both of you had spoken your minds. You may be Irish, but you are both good girls."

Casting a glance at her very curious daughter who had returned to check the meal, she said, "Louisa, explain to your father that I will not be present for dinner. I must go over to the Orphans' Home to deal with an important matter."

Dinnertime approaches as we pull up in front of the Orphans' Home. For me it is an awkward homecoming. Mr.

Rawson is delivering supplies. While I am sent inside, Mother Miles corners him in conversation.

Miss White greets me with a questioning look cast in Mother Miles' direction. "Good afternoon, Liza. This is a pleasant surprise."

I give her a pinched smile and glance frantically about for Miss Gleason. Mr. Rawson and Mother Miles enter just behind me and begin a whispered conference with Miss White. Spying Miss Gleason, I run to her and break down in tears once again. I didn't realize how much I had missed her. Why hadn't I gone to her for counsel?

Comfortingly she whispers, "Don't be impatient. 'Wait for the Lord and he will help you', Liza." (Psalm 27:14 in *Bible*)

There truly is no privacy in such a large household and soon all the little ones are surrounding me with their loving attention. To distract myself, I delight them with tales of my visit to the train station and my encounter with Jimmy selling papers.

I did not notice Miss Gleason slip away to join the other adults until Miss Jane calls everyone to dinner. Two extra chairs are placed at the table for us and it's like I never had been gone. I silently add a prayer for leniency to the mealtime grace. Amen.

I am in serious trouble, but starving. Even the condemned have a last supper, so I eat my fill of chicken stew.

Following dinner, I receive the verdict in the privacy of the front parlor.

"Liza, your behavior today has been totally unacceptable," Mother Miles says sternly. "The fact that it was motivated by Mary has helped us reflect on the best solution. We cannot lie to the Burbanks. They took you in as a favor to the Children's Friend Society. It would be a disservice to all parties concerned to continue your contract if you are not willing to serve at your best."

"Therefore, you will stay here tonight and I will discuss the matter with Mr. Burbank this afternoon. If they want you back, they may be willing to let you continue with school. Under those conditions, you will have to return."

"However, if they release you from the indenture, we will look for more suitable placement. We will find someone who can help make your dream of teaching a reality. Miss Gleason is a strong advocate for your abilities. You owe her a large debt, dear."

I silently send a grateful thank you to her, already busy teaching in the next room.

"Let us hope Mr. Burbank is a compassionate man. I'll return tomorrow morning with his answer," are Mother Miles parting words.

I sit frozen in my chair unable to move. Too much has happened this day.

God hath chosen the weak things of the world
to confound the things which are mighty.

1 Corinthians 1:27 in *Bible*

Liberty Farm, Worcester, Massachusetts. 2003.

EPILOGUE

Orphans' Home   January 21, 1853

I watch the sun rise for I cannot sleep. The newly fallen snow sparkles as the peach colored dawn fades to leave a crystal clear blue sky. How can one be sad with such a glorious beginning to the day?

Mother Miles arrives with Mr. Burbank about half past eleven to issue the verdict. Peeking out the window to read their faces, I decide their calm expressions add new hope to this most important day in my life. I fairly fly down the stairs.

"Good morning, ma'am. Good morning, sir," I curtsey politely determined to show strong character.

"Good morning, Liza," they respond in unison through clouds of foggy breath.

Quickly, they move to the chairs close to the warm fire while I help serve tea and lemon bread.

"I am greatly disturbed by your actions yesterday, Eliza," begins Mr. Burbank. "You near broke Mrs. Burbank's heart with your selfishness. However, we've decided to free you from your indenture since you are such an ungrateful child. Mrs. Miles has suggested we sign Lucy Parkhurst in your stead; and we are willing."

"F-t-t-f," I release my breath, which I didn't even realize I'd been holding. Uncontrollably, tears pool in my eyes. My body betrays my will to be strong.

A flurry of activity begins as Miss White brings Lucy in to meet Mr. Burbank. They all sign the documents and prepare Lucy for the sleigh ride to Shrewsbury. Stunned, I sit quietly in the corner near the hearth in disbelief that a solution has been found until Miss Gleason sends for me to help her with the little ones reading in the schoolroom. I beam with pride and pleasure as I leave the room. Thankfully, I remember my manners to dip a curtsey to Mr. Burbank and Mother Miles.

School room in Alcott flyer with no citation.

The following Sunday afternoon Tom and Ellen arrive in a sleigh driven by Sandy Noyes. Our family conference is a brief exchange of the news of Mary's flight to Lowell and my salvation from my indenture with the Burbanks.

Tom had already received a letter from Mary. "Tell Liza I was hired by the Boott Mills the day after I arrived. Bridgy sends her love. I board with her mother," he read.

But Mary's apology does not sit well with Tom.

Miss White explains that all is well, "The Board of Managers met to confirm the change in arrangements. Lucy Parkhurst was to have been placed in Upton this coming March with Mr. Taft, a farmer who boards the local schoolteacher.[84] Liza will take Lucy's place there, just as Lucy has taken hers in

---

[84] The Board Minutes of the Children's Friend Society reported Eliza was sent to Perley P. Taft (1805-1883) in Upton, Massachusetts on 19 March 1853, It is unknown if a schoolteacher boarded with the Tafts. Lucy Parkhurst was sent to Lee to live with the Billingham family in 1857, then to her aunt in Milford until she went to work in the Clinton Mill in1859, when she probably turned eighteen.

Shrewsbury. That way Liza may continue her education as she wishes. The future will be up to her."

Mother was right. God had opened another gate along my path just when I thought I had no choices in life. I had discovered the hard way that it is up to me to make opportunities happen by expressing my opinion, before others make choices for me. I must lift the gate latch myself. I truly believe most people try to do what is in a child's best interest, but no one can read my mind

The children I met during my stay in Worcester have shown me life is better when one's riches are shared with others, no matter how small those riches may be. Mrs. Clough showed me the warmth of family love. The Rawsons and Salisburys were generous with clothing and food for those with no families. Sarah and Pliny Earle, Emily Loveland and Abby Rawson brought Graham crackers, books and new ideas to ponder about slavery, equal rights and temperance.

The women and men who are trying to make life equal for everyone are paving a smoother path for all of us as we grow-up. Just think how Abby Rawson, Sarah Earle and Emily Loveland are already following in the footsteps of Lucy Stone and Dr. Hunt. Even though it is not easy, the girls are gaining an education to follow their chosen professions, just as I plan to do.

I do not have to do things as they've always been done before just because it is the tradition. Even little Anna Clough plans to be a hairdresser.

My life at the Orphans' Home has given me the opportunity to observe many children less fortunate than me. Some have yet to control the misfortunes placed along their path in life. Pliny Earle will never be able to speak. Will he be able to communicate outside of his family? What kind of work will he choose? Joey Williams is still at the Westboro Reformatory, unless he has run away again. Poor Becca White seems locked into the path of laundress unless she can convince her aunt to allow her to return to school. I count my blessings.

Sometimes adults hold us back by keeping us in the place they consider best, regardless of our wishes. Being an orphan changed my life. Others, no matter how well meaning, restricted my learning and work choices because I'm Irish born. Mary showed me I'm an American now. Da would expect us to seize the opportunities in our new country. I may even join Ellen and Sandy in the west. The new settlers will need teachers.

Like Miss Gleason said, "We are all humans and equal in the eyes of God. Therefore, we should be equal in the eyes of man."

Now, it is up to me to gain respect and refuse to be put down by others for I have a mind and a voice. With this bold thought, I tremble once more at the strangeness lying beyond this gate to Upton, Massachusetts.

What will my new home be like?

Taft farm location, Upton, Massachusetts. 2005.

ACKNOWLEDGEMENTS

The foundation for this novel began in 1991 at the Schlesinger Library with a National Endowment for the Humanities "New Scholarship on Women" Fellowship and built upon as a 1997 Lila Wallace-Reader's Digest Teacher Fellow at the American Antiquarian Society. Along the way I encountered several children living in Worcester, Massachusetts whose lives were touched by the call for reform. Motivated by questions from students of all ages, especially my students at Auburn Middle School in Auburn, Massachusetts, I endeavored to better understand this dynamic era leading up to the Civil War, which is often superficially addressed by many secondary teachers. Every ranger, docent and workshop leader at Old Sturbridge Village, Lowell National Historic Park and Blackstone River Valley National Heritage Corridor helped my students and I "step" into the 19th century.

I could not have produced this work without the encouragement, suggestions and assistance of the staffs of the American Antiquarian Society and the Worcester Historical Museum; history room librarian at the Worcester Public Library Nancy Gaudette; the Upton Historical Society; members of the American Association of University Women-Worcester Branch, the Worcester History Group and the Worcester Women's History Project; and my friends, students and relatives. I especially wish to thank the following people who helped me lay the groundwork for this novel: my niece Lily Board, my nephew Jason Kramer, Cindy and Beth Randall, Beth and Elizabeth Hetrick, Kendra Underwood, and Elizabeth Kapas DiPetro.

I greatly appreciate the second wave of constructive criticism every first writer needs from the Auburn Middle School eighth grade Diamond Team of 2000, Kim Coulombe, the Milford Writer's Workshop, Jane Budzyna, Pat and Kathryn Pezzella, and Dr. Richard Giziowski. The following people provided valuable historical insights on the work: Albert B. Southwick, Dr. John McClymer, Dr. Jeanette Greenwood, James D. Moran, Dr. Thomas Doughton, and Dr. Carolyn Howe. A special thank you goes to Hannah Geshelin who kicked the project back on the front burner in 2002.

After a ten year hiatus the freedom of my retirement schedule, encouragement of Art and Jo Kramer and my eldest son Chris' development of my 2012 website *Window on Your Past* at www.windowonyourpast.com/site moved me to publish.

This production could not have been accomplished without the love, support and understanding of my husband Nick Moran, my children: Chris and Kathy Donoghue Moran, Wes and Laura Hesse Moran, and my grandchildren Jared and Jocelyn Moran who at the same age as Liza must choose which gates to open along their path of life. Finally I thank my father Clayton C. Board, my mother Virginia Lee Larsen Board, and my maternal grandfather George Larsen for encouraging me to observe and appreciate the world, both present and past.

19TH CENTURY GLOSSARY

The following definitions and pronunciations are from either: *Webster's School Dictionary.* Springfield, MA: Merriam-Webster, 1986 or *Merriam-Webster's Collegiate Dictionary,* Springfield, MA: Merriam-Webster, 1998.

<u>Pronunciation guide:</u>　　　' = stressed syllable

ä = cot, cart

e = pet

ē = easy

ə = abut

ī = life

ō = bone

ü = food

abodes - a place to live

advocacy- ['ad-və-ka-sē] supporting a cause

agrarian- farming interests

analogy- a similarity

appendages- dependent people; not the main body like arms

apprentice- one who works for an experienced employer to learn a trade

arbitrary- decisions based on individual preference, often not based on the facts

avocations- interests pursued especially for enjoyment; hobby

beau- ['bō] sweetheart

beef gall- made by soaking beef liver in water

behold'n- beholden; to owe someone for a favor of debt

benefactress- woman who is helpful

benevolence- [be-'nev-ləns or 'nə-va] an act of kindness

benevolent- desiring to do good for others

betrothal- engaged to be married

bluing- a blue color added to rinse water to prevent yellowing

boarders- As people searched for better economic opportunities, cities were full of semi-nomadic, unskilled and property-less men and women. Often families who owned homes would rent out one or more rooms. This was mutually beneficial. The extra income helped pay the owner's mortgage while the boarder received a room and meals along with a sense of family.

boisterously- noisily or rowdy

bound out- see indenture

burdensome- a problem

cachou- ['ka-shü or ka-'shü] lozenges, catechu; pills to sweeten one's breathe. Oliver Chase built the first lozenge machine in 1847. The lozenge of gum arabic, peppermint and brown sugar at a Boston apothecary's shop became Necco wafers.

caldron- big kettle or pot of boiling water

calico- cotton cloth with a colored pattern printed on one side

carpetbag- valise or suitcase made of carpet with leather handles

chaperone- an older or married person who attends to a younger woman to protect her

cobbled- paved with rounded stones larger than a pebble and smaller than a boulder

colleen- Irish girl

comfits- ['kəm(p)-fət or 'käm (p)-fət] hard candies used to keep children, and sometimes adults, comfortable during long church service; usually sugar coated fruit, root (licorice), nuts or seeds

common- an area of land in the center of a town used by all the people in the community

condemned- pronounced guilty of wrong doing

confectionary- a store selling candy and sweets

conference- a meeting to exchange opinions

constable- police man

counsel- to give advice

convention- an assembly of persons met for a common purpose

cordial- a medicine that stimulates the heart; usually contains alcohol

countenance- facial expression

crack-brained- someone who's behavior is erratic or not stable

crankshaft- a bar used to transfer power or motion by rotating rods attached to an engine

cypher- cipher; do arithmetic or mathematical calculations

daguerreotype- [də-'ger-ē-ə-tīp] early photograph; developed by L.J. M. Daguerre in France in 1839.

deacons- ['dē-kəns] church leaders who help minister

debtor- one who owes money

dejectedly- sadly

democratic - a government where the people have equal representation in running it

demurely- not extreme; shyly; ladylike

destitute - penniless

dilemma- problem

diligently- make steady and energetic effort

disembark-getting off a ship or train

dolt- [dōlt] a stupid person

domestic- a hired household servant. The average wage for a female domestic was $1.50 per week with board (a room and meals) according to the 1850 Census for Worcester.

domestic- at home

donned- put on

drawers- underwear

drudge - one who labors at hard, uninteresting and distasteful tasks for others

ebony- [ˈeb-ə-nē] dark black color resembling the wood from the ebony tree

endeavors- to work for a goal or make an effort

enlighten- to give knowledge or more information

epidemic- affecting a large number of people

errant - going against accepted behavior.

expectation- something one looks forward to or hopes for

famine- a time when no food is available

forum- a public place for discussion

Free Soiler- a third political party formed in 1848 by radical abolitionists when both major party presidential candidates favored continuation of slavery. The fear was slavery would be allowed in the new western territories.

frigid- cold

frock- dress

fugitives- runaways

gallant- a fashionable young man in dress or bearing; polite and attentive to women

Garrisonians- people who agree with William Lloyd Garrison calling for immediate freeing of the slaves, women's rights, temperance, pacifism and other causes.

gender- sex; male or female

generalities- vague or inadequate ideas based on a large sample rather than being specific

Gibraltars- delicate white candies flavored with lemon or peppermint. A Mrs. Spencer began making them as she had in England after being shipwrecked and landing in Salem, Massachusetts in 1822.

gold fields-gold was discovered in California in 1849 at Sutter's Mill.

grist mill- a place to grind grain into meal: flour, oatmeal, corn meal

ground work- foundation or base

guardianship- legally responsible for care of a person or property

hack- hackney; a horse drawn cab for hire

herbal- ['ər-bal] relating to plants especially when used for medicine

hoop- petticoat with wire hoops stitched on it as a frame to hold skirts away from the body. They replaced the heavy (sometimes fifteen pounds) usual seven layers of petticoats in fashion in the mid19th century. They were manufactured in Worcester, Massachusetts by Icabod Washburn beginning in 1851.

hygiene- ['hī-jēn] how to preserve of one's health

immoral- without good character; someone who does not follow the behavior standards of their day

impertinence- rude; outside the accepted behavior

impressive- the power of making or tending to excite attention, awe or admiration

indenture- a contract by which a person is bound into service for a specific length of time

indentured servants- people who sign an agreement to work for a master for several years for room and **bound out** board, but little or no pay; children usually served until 18 years of age

Indian summer- a period of mild weather in late autumn or early winter

industrial- work done by machines rather than hand; usually refers to manufacturing rather than agriculture, craftsmanship or trade

intemperate- one who drinks too much alcohol and cannot control oneself

intolerance- not willing to grant equal treatment to someone who is not like you in looks or beliefs

intoxicating- something that makes one drunk or unable to control oneself

jangled- harsh, often ringing sound

jostling- pushing and shoving

keep- food, shelter and sometimes clothing

kittle- kettle

legislators- lawmakers

leniency- easy, less harsh

levies- ['lev-ēs] places a tax on something or someone

liberal- open minded to new ideas

linsey-woolsey- a coarse fabric woven with a linen warp and woolen weft; it is warm and sturdy, but considered poor quality

lithograph- a print made by inking an etched picture on a stone or metal plate; used in newspapers, magazines and books before photos could be reproduced

Lucifer match- a wooden friction match

lunatics- people unable to control themselves; insane

Lyceum- [lī-'sē-əm] a group who meet for discussion and popular instruction through lectures

machinist- In 1831 Daniel Webster described a mechanic as "a person whose occupation is to construct machines, or goods, wares, instruments, furniture and the like."

mannequin- a model of the human body

mantel- a shelf above a fireplace

manufactured- made a finished product from raw materials

mass- a Catholic church service.

midwifery- practice of assisting women in child birth

morality- good behavior according to societies rules; chaste

mute- cannot speak

narrative- words that tell a story

nary- not any

necessary- outdoor toilet; out house or privy

negotiate- discuss with another to arrive at an agreement

nest egg- a fund of money saved for as a reserve

ninny- ['nin-ē] a fool or simpleton

nun- a woman belonging to a religious order usually under
        vows of poverty, obedience and chastity

omnibus- a horse drawn wagon carrying many passenger
        around town

orphans- children without parents

ould sod- old land or homeland; referring to Ireland

pantelettes - long under drawers with a frill or other finish at
        the bottom of each leg that extend below   the dress;
        the crotch seam was not stitched closed as it is today

papist- ['pā-pəst] a negative term for a Roman Catholic as a
        follower of the Pope

peat- blocks of sod or turf dried for fuel or used as building
        blocks

petition- to ask or make a request

phrenologist- [fri-'näl-ə-jest] a person who examines the
        shape and prominent places on a person's skull and
        from the bumps, supposedly determines what mental
        faculties and   character traits that person possesses. It
        was a hot topic beginning in the 1830s.

physiology- [fiz-ē-'äl-ə-jē] the study of the parts and functions
        of a living organism

piece work- a job that pays for each item completed

piston- a sliding piece moved by pressure

plight- a difficult situation

pnnmony [pneumonia]- inflammation of the lungs

popular sovereignty- right of the people of a new territory to decide by vote whether to allow slavery or not

precarious- [pri-'kar-ē-əs] dangerous

prim - neat and well mannered

privy - privately given information

Prods- English Protestants who were not tolerant of Irish Catholics

promiscuous- an audience or group with men and women mixed together

rabble rousers- people who stir up groups of people especially to hatred or violence

radicals- people who are extreme or outside the usual or traditional behavior or beliefs

recitation- a lesson spoken aloud in front of the class either from memory or in response to assigned questions.

recourse- a source of help

reformers- people who try to improve society

reformatory- a jail for young or first offenders to provide training and change their behaviors

refuge- safe shelter

relict- a widow

remanded- ordered back

resolutions- formal expressions of the opinion to solve a problem or state the purpose of a group

resolved- the act of forming an opinion

retorted- answered back angrily or quickly

reveries- daydreams

root cellar- a pit for storage, especially root crops like potatoes

salvation- deliverance from sin or danger

seminary- a school for higher learning

servitude clause- part of the law dealing with responsibility to serve a master

shiftless- lazy

signed- used sign language

slovenly- lazy

smoothin' iron- a pressing iron used to take the wrinkles out of fabric

solace- to soothe or calm

specie- ['spē–shē] money made of gold or silver, not paper. It was known as 'hard' cash.

spinster- an unmarried woman who before the Industrial Revolution would sit and spin thread or yarn on a spinning wheel

stagnation- stale or not moving forward

suffrage- the right to vote

'sumption [consumption]- tuberculosis; a wasting away of the lungs

swaddled- wrapped

sweat shop- a workshop with low wages, long hours and unfavorable conditions

swine- pigs

temperance- moderation or refusal to use alcoholic beverages

tenement- crowded apartment building in a poor section of town

textiles- woven cloth or the fibers that are used to make cloth

thatched- roof made of straw or rushes

tradition- the way something is always done

traitor- a person who betrays a trust

Turkish Delight- a jellylike or gummy candy dusted in with sugar

typhoid- a contagious disease caused by bacteria with severe
　　　flu like symptoms
tyrants- people who abuse their power

Utopia; utopian- a community that tries to be perfect
unquenchable- cannot be put out

vain- worthless; unsuccessful
valise- [və-'lēs] see carpetbag
verdict- judgment or decision
vital- of utmost importance
vocational- relating to skill or trade needed for a career

wee'ns- wee ones; little children
whims- sudden idea
wooing- winning a lady's affection and usually her hand in
　　　marriage
wretchedness- distressed in mind or body

ye- you

NOTE OTHER WORDS YOU HAD TO LOOK UP BELOW:

BIBLIOGRAPHY

1850 United States Census for Worcester County at American Antiquarian Society, Worcester, MA and at Ancestry.com (2012).

Alcott, William A. *The Young Woman's Book of Health*. Boston: Tappan, Whittemore and Mason, 1850.

American Antiquarian Society, Worcester, MA. <www.americanantiquarian.org>.

"Another 'Sensible Woman'", *Massachusetts Cataract and Waterfall*, Vol. 8 No. 34. 7 November 1850 (135) at American Antiquarian Society, Worcester, MA.

Bacon, Margaret Hope. *I Speak for My Slave Sister: The Life of Abigail Kelley Foster*. NY: Crowell, 1974. (Young Adult Book)

Baker, Carlos. *Emerson Among the Eccentrics*. NY: Viking, 1996.

Bryant, Jennifer Fisher. *Lucretia Mott: A Guiding Light*. Grand Rapids, MI: William B. Eerdmans, 1996. (Juvenile Book)

Cayleff, Susan E. *Wash and Be Healed, The Water-Cure Movement and Women's Health.* Philadelphia: Temple University Press, 1987.

Chase, Charles A. "Nobility Hill," *Proceedings of Worcester Society of the Antiquities*. 8 December 1908, (231-246) at American Antiquarian Society, Worcester, MA.

Children's Friend Society Ledger at American Antiquarian Society, Worcester, MA.

The Citizen's And Stranger's Guide In the City of Worcester Containing A Safe Directory To The Best Business Establishments in the City. Worcester: H. J. Howland. Dated at 1848.

Coffey, Michael, ed. *The Irish in America.* NY: Hyperion, 1997.

Davis, S. H. "Sketches By the Way," *The Ladies' Album,* Volume XV. Boston: Davis, 1850.

Dickens, Charles. *American Notes.* Gloucester, MA: Peter Smith, 1842.

Diner, Hasia R. *Erin's Daughters in American: Irish Immigrant Women in the Nineteenth Century.* Baltimore: Johns Hopkins University Press, 1983.

Dublin Thomas. *Women at Work: The Transformation of Work and Community in Lowell, Massachusetts, 1826-1860.* NY: Columbia University Press, 1979.

Earle, Pliney, comp. *The Earle Family Ralph Earle and his Descendants.* Worcester: Press of Charles Hamilton, 1888 at American Antiquarian Society, Worcester, MA. [by the uncle, not our character]

Evans, Jo, Ed. *Ultimate Visual Dictionary.* New York: Dorling Kindersley Limited, 1994.

Eisler, Benita, ed. *The Lowell Offering.* NY: W.W. Norton and Company, 1977.

Farnum, Elmer F. *The Quickest Route: The History of the Norwich & Worcester Railroad.* Chester, CT: Pequot Press, 1973.

"The Gentler Sex," *Massachusetts Cataract and Waterfall,* Vol. 8 No. 35. 14 November 1850 at American Antiquarian, Worcester, MA..

Grolier. *The Book of Popular Science*, Volume 4. New York: Grolier Inc, 1976.

Hale, Edward Everett (penciled in). *Worcester in 1850.* Worcester: Henry J. Howland, 1850.

The Heart of the Commonwealth: or Worcester As It Is. Worcester: Henry J. Howland, 1856.

Hoffert, Sylvia D. *When Hens Crow: The Women's Rights Movements In Antebellum America.* Bloomington, IN: Indiana University Press, 1995.

Howland, Henry J. *Worcester Almanac Directory and Business Advertiser for 1850. Worcester: Henry J. Howland, 1850* at American Antiquarian Society and at Ancestry.com (2012).

Howland, Henry J. *Worcester Almanac Directory and Business Advertiser for 1851. Worcester: Henry J. Howland, 1851* at American Antiquarian Society and at Ancestry.com (2012).

James, Edward; James, Janet; Boyer, Paul, eds. *Notable American Women, 1607-1950.* Cambridge: Harvard University Press, 1971. (3 volumes)

Jewett's *The Youth's Temperance Lecturer* (1841) at American Antiquarian Society, Worcester, MA.

Keck-Henderson, Ann. *"most pleasant rooms to live in"* Worcester, MA: Worcester Historical Museum, 1982-1983.

Kerr, Andrea Moore. *Lucy Stone: Speaking Out for Equality.* NJ: Rutgers University Press, 1992.

Knowlton, Eliot B. and Gibson-Quigley, Sandra, eds. *Worcester's Best.* Worcester: Preservation Worcester, 1996.

Kolmerten, Carol. *The American Life of Ernestine L. Rose.* Syracuse University Press, 1999.

Lacour-Gayet, Robert. *Everyday Life in the United States Before the Civil War, 1830-1860.* NY: Frederick Ungar Publishing Company, 1969.

Lawes, Carolyn Jo. "Public Women, Public Lives: Women in Worcester, Massachusetts, 1818-1860." Ph.D. Thesis, University of California, Davis, 1992.

----- *Women and Reform in a New England Community, 1815-1860.* Lexington: University Press of Kentucky, 2000.

Lincoln, William. *Worcester in 1850.* Worcester: Henry J. Howland, Jan 1850, Free eBook at <books.google.com>.

Lyrics Mania. <www.lyricsmania.com> (2012).

Mayer, Henry. *All on Fire: William Lloyd Garrison and the Abolition of Slavery.* New York: St. Martin's Griffin, 1998.

McClymer, John. *This High and Holy Moment: The First National Woman's Rights Convention, Worcester, 1850.* Orlando, FL: Harcourt Brace, 1999.

McGuffey's *Second Eclectic Reader.* New York: Van Nostrand Reinhold Company, Inc., 1879.

McKissack, Patricia and Fredrick. *Sojourner Truth, Ain't I a Woman?* New York: Scholastic, 1992. (Young Adult Book)

McPherson, Stephanie Sammartino. *I Speak For the Women: A Story About Lucy Stone.* Minneapolis: Carolrhoda Books, 1992. (Young Adult Book)

Meyer, Susan M. *The Salisbury Mansion: A Plan for Furnishings.* Worcester, MA: Worcester Historical Museum, 1986.

Morse, Minna. "Facing a Bumpy History." *Smithsonian,* October 1997.

National Aegis. 23 October 1850 at American Antiquarian Society, Worcester, MA.

Paine, Nathaniel. *Memoir of Stephen Salisbury.* Reprinted from the proceedings of the Massachusetts Historical Society, June 1906.

Pathfinder Railway Guide. Boston: Snow U. Wilder, 1850.

Salisbury Family Papers at American Antiquarian Society, Worcester, MA.

Sandrof, Ivan. *Massachusetts Towns: An 1840 View.* Barre, MA: Barre Publishers, 1963.

Sigerman, Harriet. *The Young Oxford History of Women in the United States.* NY: Oxford University Press, 1995. (11 volumes)

Southwick, Albert. *More Once Told Tales of Worcester County.* Worcester: Databooks, 1994.

Stanton, Elizabeth Cady, Susan B. Anthony, and Matilda Joslyn Gage, ed. *History of Woman Suffrage.* NY: Fowler & Wells, 1881.

Steinfeld, Robert. *The Invention of Free Labor.* Chapel Hill: University of North Carolina Press, 1991.

Staples, S.E., compiler. *Worcester Children's Friend Society, 1849-1884.* Worcester, 1884.

Sterling, Dorothy. *Ahead of Her Time, Abby Kelley and the Politics of Antislavery.* NY: W.W. Norton, 1991.

"The Gentler Sex," *The Massachusetts Waterfall and Cataract* 14 November 1850 (135) at American Antiquarian Society, Worcester, MA.

The Worcester Magazine. January 1908. Worcester Public Library, Worcester, MA.

Tymeson, Mildred McClary. *Worcester Centennial, 1848-1948.* Worcester: Worcester Centennial, Inc., 1948.

Uchikata, H. M. "Thesis on the Worcester Children's Friend Society". University of Washington, Seattle in Sociology in 1918.

The Unitarian Congregational Register for the Year 1850. Boston: William Crosby and H. P. Nichols, 1850.

Untermeyer, Louis. *A Century Of Candymaking 1847-1947.* Boston: Barta Press, 1947.

Voss, Frederick S. *Majestic in His Wrath: Pictorial Life of Frederick Douglass.* Washington: Smithsonian Institution Press, 1995.

Wall, Caleb A. *Reminiscences of Worcester.* Worcester, MA: Tyler & Seagrave, 1877.

Wallace, Irving. *The Fabulous Showman.* NY: Knopf, 1959.

Watts, Rev. Isaac. *Divine and Moral Songs for Children.* London: George Routledge and Sons, 1878.

Worcester Anti-Slavery Sewing Circle Record Book, 1839-1857 at Worcester Historical Museum.

Worcester Daily Spy. 24 October 1850 at American Antiquarian Society, Worcester, MA.

Worcester Art Museum. Worcester, MA. <www.worcesterart.org>.

Worcester Historical Museum. Worcester, MA. <www.worcesterhistory.org>.

Worcester Women's History Project for 1850 National Woman's Rights Convention Proceedings and related documents. <www.wwhp.org/Resources> (2012).

Yess, Thomas. "Shrewsbury Street Newspaper Clippings" at Worcester Historical Museum.

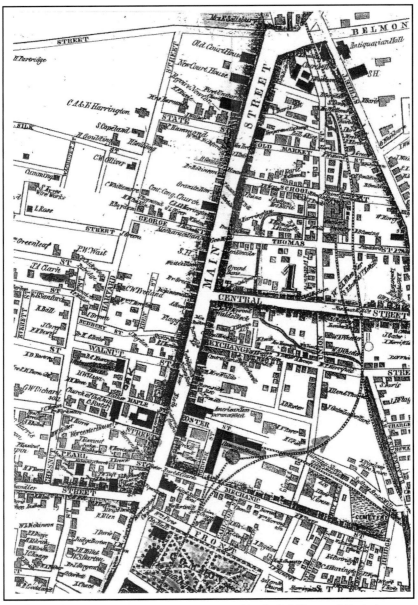

Top Left: Salisbury Mansion   Far Left: Miles and Earle homes
Bottom left: Common and Station   Far Right: Orphans' Home
Bottom right: Loveland and Clough homes and Washington Square

THE SETTING OF OUR STORY

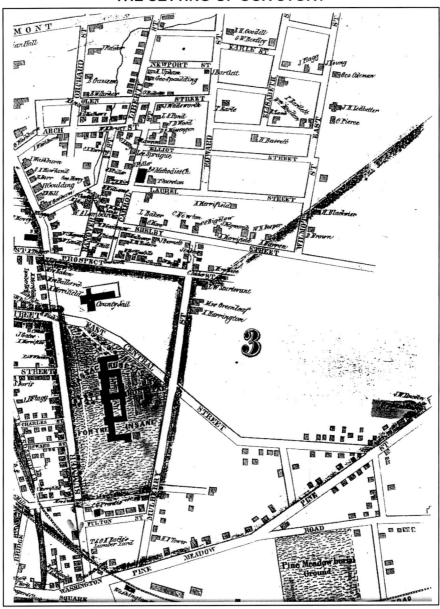

Excerpt from Map of City of Worcester, Worcester County, Massachusetts.
From original survey by H. F. Walling. Published by Warren Lazell, 1851.
From collections of the Worcester Historical Museum.